Business Intelligence
and Data Mining

Business Intelligence and Data Mining

Anil K. Maheshwari, PhD

 BUSINESS EXPERT PRESS

First published by
Business Expert Press, LLC
222 East 46th Street, New York, NY 10017
www.businessexpertpress.com

ISBN-13: 978-1-63157-120-6 (print)
ISBN-13: 978-1-63157-121-3 (e-book)

eISSN: 2333-6757
ISSN: 2333-6749

Business Expert Press Big Data and Business Analytics Collection.

Cover and interior design by S4Carlisle Publishing Services Private Ltd.,
Chennai, India

Dedicated to my parents,
Mr. Ratan Lal and Mrs. Meena Maheshwari.

Abstract

Business is the act of doing something productive to serve someone's needs, and thus earn a living, and make the world a better place. Business activities are recorded on paper or using electronic media, and then these records become data. There is more data from customers' responses and on the industry as a whole. All this data can be analyzed and mined using special tools and techniques to generate patterns and intelligence, which reflect how the business is functioning. These ideas can then be fed back into the business so that it can evolve to become more effective and efficient in serving customer needs. And the cycle continues on.

Business intelligence includes tools and techniques for data gathering, analysis, and visualization for helping with executive decision making in any industry. Data mining includes statistical and machine-learning techniques to build decision-making models from raw data. Data mining techniques covered in this book include decision trees, regression, artificial neural networks, cluster analysis, and many more. Text mining, web mining, and big data are also covered in an easy way. A primer on data modeling is included for those uninitiated in this topic.

Keywords

Data Analytics, Data Mining, Business Intelligence, Decision Trees, Regression, Neural Networks, Cluster analysis, Association rules.

Contents

Preface

There are many good textbooks in the market on *Business Intelligence and Data Mining*. So, why should anyone write another book on this topic? I have been teaching courses in business intelligence and data mining for a few years. More recently, I have been teaching this course to combined classes of MBA and Computer Science students. Existing textbooks seem too long, too technical, and too complex for use by students. This book fills a need for an accessible book on the topic of business intelligence and data mining. My goal was to write a conversational book that feels easy and informative. This is an easy book that covers everything important, with concrete examples, and invites the reader to join this field.

This book has developed from my own class notes. It reflects many years of IT industry experience, as well as many years of academic teaching experience. The chapters are organized for a typical one-semester graduate course. The book contains caselets from real-world stories at the beginning of every chapter. There is a running case study across the chapters as exercises.

Many thanks are in order. My father Mr. Ratan Lal Maheshwari encouraged me to put my thoughts in writing and make a book out of them. My wife Neerja helped me find the time and motivation to write this book. My brother, Dr. Sunil Maheshwari, and I have had many years of encouraging conversations about it. My colleague Dr. Edi Shivaji provided help and advice during my teaching the BIDM courses. Another colleague Dr. Scott Herriott served as a role model as an author of many textbooks. Our assistant Ms. Karen Slowick at Maharishi University of Management (MUM) proofread the first draft of this book. Dean Dr. Greg Guthrie at MUM provided many ideas and ways to disseminate the book. Ms. Adri-Mari Vilonel in South Africa helped create an opportunity to use this book at a corporate MBA program.

Thanks are due also to my many students at MUM and elsewhere who proved good partners in my learning more about this area. Finally, thanks to Maharishi Mahesh Yogi for providing a wonderful university, MUM, where students develop their intellect as well as their consciousness.

Dr. Anil K. Maheshwari
Fairfield, IA
December 2014.

CHAPTER 1

Wholeness of Business Intelligence and Data Mining

Business is the act of doing something productive to serve someone's needs, and thus earn a living and make the world a better place. Business activities are recorded on paper or using electronic media, and then these records become data. There is more data from customers' responses and on the industry as a whole. All this data can be analyzed and mined using special tools and techniques to generate patterns and intelligence, which reflect how the business is functioning. These ideas can then be fed back into the business so that it can evolve to become more effective and efficient in serving customer needs. And the cycle continues on (Figure 1.1).

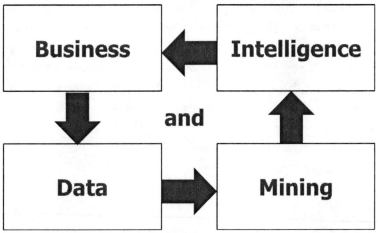

Figure 1.1 Business intelligence and data mining cycle

Business Intelligence

Any business organization needs to continually monitor its business environment and its own performance, and then rapidly adjust its future plans. This includes monitoring the industry, the competitors, the suppliers, and the customers. The organization needs to also develop a balanced scorecard to track its own health and vitality. Executives typically determine what they want to track based on their key performance Indexes (KPIs) or key result areas (KRAs). Customized reports need to be designed to deliver the required information to every executive. These reports can be converted into customized dashboards that deliver the information rapidly and in easy-to-grasp formats.

Caselet: MoneyBall—Data Mining in Sports

Analytics in sports was made popular by the book and movie, Moneyball. Statistician Bill James and Oakland A's General Manager Billy Bean placed emphasis on crunching numbers and data instead of watching an athlete's style and looks. Their goal was to make a team better while using fewer resources. The key action plan was to pick important role players at a lower cost while avoiding the famous players who demand higher salaries but may provide a low return on a team's investment. Rather than relying on the scouts' experience and intuition Bean selected players based almost exclusively on their on-base percentage (OBP). By finding players with a high OBP but, with characteristics that lead scouts to dismiss them, Bean assembled a team of undervalued players with far more potential than the A's hamstrung finances would otherwise allow.

Using this strategy, they proved that even small market teams can be competitive—a case in point, the Oakland A's. In 2004, two years after adopting the same sabermetric model, the Boston Red Sox won their first World Series since 1918. (Source: Moneyball 2004)

Q1. *Could similar techniques apply to the games of soccer, or cricket? If so, how?*

Q2. *What are the general lessons from this story?*

Business intelligence is a broad set of information technology (IT) solutions that includes tools for gathering, analyzing, and reporting information to the users about performance of the organization and its environment. These IT solutions are among the most highly prioritized solutions for investment.

Consider a retail business chain that sells many kinds of goods and services around the world, online and in physical stores. It generates data about sales, purchases, and expenses from multiple locations and time frames. Analyzing this data could help identify fast-selling items, regional-selling items, seasonal items, fast-growing customer segments, and so on. It might also help generate ideas about what products sell together, which people tend to buy which products, and so on. These insights and intelligence can help design better promotion plans, product bundles, and store layouts, which in turn lead to a better-performing business.

The vice president of sales of a retail company would want to track the sales to date against monthly targets, the performance of each store and product category, and the top store managers that month. The vice president of finance would be interested in tracking daily revenue, expense, and cash flows by store; comparing them against plans; measuring cost of capital; and so on.

Pattern Recognition

A pattern is a design or model that helps grasp something. Patterns help connect things that may not appear to be connected. Patterns help cut through complexity and reveal simpler understandable trends. Patterns can be as definitive as hard scientific rules, like the rule that the sun always rises in the east. They can also be simple generalizations, such as the Pareto principle, which states that 80 percent of effects come from 20 percent of the causes.

A perfect pattern or model is one that (a) accurately describes a situation, (b) is broadly applicable, and (c) can be described in a simple manner. $E = MC^2$ would be such a *general*, *accurate*, and *simple* (GAS) model. Very often, all three qualities are not achievable in a single model, and one has to settle for two of three qualities in the model.

Patterns can be temporal, which is something that regularly occurs over time. Patterns can also be spatial, such as things being organized in a certain way. Patterns can be functional, in that doing certain things leads to certain effects. Good patterns are often symmetric. They echo basic structures and patterns that we are already aware of.

A temporal rule would be that "some people are always late," no matter what the occasion or time. Some people may be aware of this pattern and some may not be. Understanding a pattern like this would help dissipate a lot of unnecessary frustration and anger. One can just joke that some people are born "10 minutes late," and laugh it away. Similarly, Parkinson's law states that works expands to fill up all the time available to do it.

A spatial pattern, following the 80–20 rule, could be that the top 20 percent of customers lead to 80 percent of the business. Or 20 percent of products generate 80 percent of the business. Or 80 percent of incoming customer service calls are related to just 20 percent of the products. This last pattern may simply reveal a discrepancy between a product's features and what the customers believe about the product. The business can then decide to invest in educating the customers better so that the customer service calls can be significantly reduced.

A functional pattern may involve test-taking skills. Some students perform well on essay-type questions. Others do well in multiple-choice questions. Yet other students excel in doing hands-on projects, or in oral presentations. An awareness of such a pattern in a class of students can help the teacher design a balanced testing mechanism that is fair to all.

Retaining students is an ongoing challenge for universities. Recent data-based research shows that students leave a school for social reasons more than they do for academic reasons. This pattern/insight can instigate schools to pay closer attention to students engaging in extracurricular activities and developing stronger bonds at school. The school can invest in entertainment activities, sports activities, camping trips, and other activities. The school can also begin to actively gather data about every student's participation in those activities, to predict at-risk students and take corrective action.

However, long-established patterns can also be broken. The past cannot always predict the future. A pattern like "all swans are white" does not mean that there may not be a black swan. Once enough anomalies are discovered, the underlying pattern itself can shift. The economic meltdown in 2008 to 2009 was because of the collapse of the accepted pattern, that is, "housing prices always go up." A deregulated financial environment made markets more volatile and led to greater swings in markets, leading to the eventual collapse of the entire financial system.

Diamond mining is the act of digging into large amounts of unrefined ore to discover precious gems or nuggets. Similarly, data mining is the act of digging into large amounts of raw data to discover unique nontrivial useful patterns. Data is cleaned up, and then special tools and techniques can be applied to search for patterns. Diving into clean and nicely organized data from the right perspectives can increase the chances of making the right discoveries.

A skilled diamond miner knows what a diamond looks like. Similarly, a skilled data miner should know what kinds of patterns to look for. The patterns are essentially about what hangs together and what is separate. Therefore, knowing the business domain well is very important. It takes knowledge and skill to discover the patterns. It is like finding a needle in a haystack. Sometimes the pattern may be hiding in plain sight. At other times, it may take a lot of work, and looking far and wide, to find surprising useful patterns. Thus, a systematic approach to mining data is necessary to efficiently reveal valuable insights.

For instance, the attitude of employees toward their employer may be hypothesized to be determined by a large number of factors, such as level of education, income, tenure in the company, and gender. It may be surprising if the data reveals that the attitudes are determined first and foremost by their age bracket. Such a simple insight could be powerful in designing organizations effectively. The data miner has to be open to any and all possibilities.

When used in clever ways, data mining can lead to interesting insights and be a source of new ideas and initiatives. One can predict the traffic pattern on highways from the movement of cell phone (in the car) locations on the highway. If the locations of cell phones on a highway or roadway are not moving fast enough, it may be a sign of traffic congestion. Telecom companies can thus provide real-time traffic information to the drivers on their cell phones, or on their GPS devices, without the need of any video cameras or traffic reporters.

Similarly, organizations can find out an employee's arrival time at the office by when their cell phone shows up in the parking lot. Observing the record of the swipe of the parking permit card in the company parking garage can inform the organization whether an employee is in the office building or out of the office at any moment in time.

Some patterns may be so sparse that a very large amount of diverse data has to be seen together to notice any connections. For instance, locating the debris of a flight that may have vanished midcourse would require bringing together data from many sources, such as satellites, ships, and navigation systems. The raw data may come with various levels of quality, and may even be conflicting. The data at hand may or may not be adequate for finding good patterns. Additional dimensions of data may need to be added to help solve the problem.

Data Processing Chain

Data is the new natural resource. Implicit in this statement is the recognition of hidden value in data. Data lies at the heart of business intelligence. There is a sequence of steps to be followed to benefit from the data in a systematic way. Data can be modeled and stored in a database. Relevant data can be extracted from the operational data stores according to certain reporting and analyzing purposes, and stored in a data warehouse. The data from the warehouse can be combined with other sources of data, and mined using data mining techniques to generate new insights. The insights need to be visualized and communicated to the right audience in real time for competitive advantage. Figure 1.2 explains the progression of data processing activities. The rest of this chapter will cover these five elements in the data processing chain.

Data

Anything that is recorded is data. Observations and facts are data. Anecdotes and opinions are also data, of a different kind. Data can be numbers, such as the record of daily weather or daily sales. Data can be alphanumeric, such as the names of employees and customers.

Figure 1.2 Data processing chain

1. Data could come from any number of sources. It could come from operational records inside an organization, and it can come from records compiled by the industry bodies and government agencies. Data could come from individuals telling stories from memory and from people's interaction in social contexts. Data could come from machines reporting their own status or from logs of web usage.

2. Data can come in many ways. It may come as paper reports. It may come as a file stored on a computer. It may be words spoken over the phone. It may be e-mail or chat on the Internet. It may come as movies and songs in DVDs, and so on.

3. There is also data about data. It is called metadata. For example, people regularly upload videos on YouTube. The format of the video file (whether it was a high-def file or lower resolution) is metadata. The information about the time of uploading is metadata. The account from which it was uploaded is also metadata. The record of downloads of the video is also metadata.

Data can be of different types.

1. Data could be an unordered collection of values. For example, a retailer sells shirts of red, blue, and green colors. There is no intrinsic ordering among these color values. One can hardly argue that any one color is higher or lower than the other. This is called nominal (means names) data.

2. Data could be ordered values like small, medium, and large. For example, the sizes of shirts could be extra-small, small, medium, and large. There is clarity that medium is bigger than small, and large is bigger than medium. But the differences may not be equal. This is called ordinal (ordered) data.

3. Another type of data has discrete numeric values defined in a certain range, with the assumption of equal distance between the values. Customer satisfaction score may be ranked on a 10-point scale with 1 being lowest and 10 being highest. This requires the respondent to carefully calibrate the entire range as objectively as possible and place his or her own measurement in that scale. This is called interval (equal intervals) data.

4. The highest level of numeric data is ratio data that can take on any numeric value. The weights and heights of all employees would be exact numeric values. The price of a shirt will also take any numeric value. It is called ratio (any fraction) data.

5. There is another kind of data that does not lend itself to much mathematical analysis, at least not directly. Such data needs to be first structured and then analyzed. This includes data like audio, video, and graphs files, often called BLOBs (Binary Large Objects). These kinds of data lend themselves to different forms of analysis and mining. Songs can be described as happy or sad, fast-paced or slow, and so on. They may contain sentiment and intention, but these are not quantitatively precise.

The precision of analysis increases as data becomes more numeric. Ratio data could be subjected to rigorous mathematical analysis. For example, precise weather data about temperature, pressure, and humidity can be used to create rigorous mathematical models that can accurately predict future weather.

Data may be publicly available and sharable, or it may be marked private. Traditionally, the law allows the right to privacy concerning one's personal data. There is a big debate on whether the personal data shared on social media conversations is private or can be used for commercial purposes.

Datafication is a new term that means that almost every phenomenon is now being observed and stored. More devices are connected to the Internet. More people are constantly connected to "the grid," by their phone network or the Internet, and so on. Every click on the web, and every movement of the mobile devices, is being recorded. Machines are generating data. The "Internet of things" is growing faster than the Internet of people. All of this is generating an exponentially growing volume of data, at high velocity. Kryder's law predicts that the density and capability of hard drive storage media will double every 18 months. As storage costs keep coming down at a rapid rate, there is a greater incentive to record and store more events and activities at a higher resolution. Data is getting stored in more detailed resolution, and many more variables are being captured and stored.

Database

A database is a modeled collection of data that is accessible in many ways. A data model can be designed to integrate the operational data of the organization. The data model abstracts the key entities involved in an action and their relationships. Most databases today follow the relational data model and its variants. Each data modeling technique imposes rigorous rules and constraints to ensure the integrity and consistency of data over time.

Take the example of a sales organization. A data model for managing customer orders will involve data about customers, orders, products, and their interrelationships. The relationship between the customers and orders would be such that one customer can place many orders, but one order will be placed by one and only one customer. It is called a one-to-many relationship. The relationship between orders and products is a little more complex. One order may contain many products. And one product may be contained in many different orders. This is called a many-to-many relationship. Different types of relationships can be modeled in a database.

Databases have grown tremendously over time. They have grown in complexity in terms of number of the objects and their properties being recorded. They have also grown in the quantity of data being stored. A decade ago, a terabyte-sized database was considered big. Today databases are in petabytes and exabytes. Video and other media files have greatly contributed to the growth of databases. E-commerce and other web-based activities also generate huge amounts of data. Data generated through social media has also generated large databases. The e-mail archives, including attached documents of organizations, are in similar large sizes.

Many database management software systems (DBMSs) are available to help store and manage this data. These include commercial systems, such as Oracle and DB2 system. There are also open-source, free DBMS, such as MySQL and Postgres. These DBMSs help process and store millions of transactions worth of data every second.

Here is a simple database of the sales of movies worldwide for a retail organization. It shows sales transactions of movies over three quarters. Using such a file, data can be added, accessed, and updated as needed.

Movies Transaction Database				
Order #	Date sold	Product name	Location	Total value
1	April 2013	Monty Python	United States	$9
2	May 2013	Gone With the Wind	United States	$15
3	June 2013	Monty Python	India	$9
4	June 2013	Monty Python	United Kingdom	$12
5	July 2013	Matrix	United States	$12
6	July 2013	Monty Python	United States	$12
7	July 2013	Gone With the Wind	United States	$15
8	Aug 2013	Matrix	United States	$12
9	Sept 2013	Matrix	India	$12
10	Sept 2013	Monty Python	United States	$9
11	Sept 2013	Gone With the Wind	United States	$15
12	Sept 2013	Monty Python	India	$9
13	Nov 2013	Gone With the Wind	United States	$15
14	Dec 2013	Monty Python	United States	$9
15	Dec 2013	Monty Python	United States	$9

Data Warehouse

A data warehouse is an organized store of data from all over the organization, specially designed to help make management decisions. Data can be extracted from operational database to answer a particular set of queries. This data, combined with other data, can be rolled up to a consistent granularity and uploaded to a separate data store called the data warehouse. Therefore, the data warehouse is a simpler version of the operational data base, with the purpose of addressing reporting and decision-making needs only. The data in the warehouse cumulatively grows as more operational data becomes available and is extracted and appended to the data warehouse. Unlike in the operational database, the data values in the warehouse are not updated.

To create a simple data warehouse for the movies sales data, assume a simple objective of tracking sales of movies and making decisions about managing inventory. In creating this data warehouse, all the sales transaction data will be extracted from the operational data files. The data will be rolled up for all combinations of time period and product number. Thus, there will be one row for every combination of time period and product. The resulting data warehouse will look like the table what follows.

Movies Sales Data Warehouse			
Row #	Qtr Sold	Product Name	Total Value
1	Q2	Gone With the Wind	$15
2	Q2	Monty Python	$30
3	Q3	Gone With the Wind	$30
4	Q3	Matrix	$36
5	Q3	Monty Python	$30
6	Q4	Gone With the Wind	$15
7	Q4	Monty Python	$18

The data in the data warehouse is at much less detail than the transaction database. The data warehouse could have been designed at a lower or higher level of detail, or granularity. If the data warehouse were designed on a monthly level, instead of a quarterly level, there would be many more rows of data. When the number of transactions approaches millions and higher, with dozens of attributes in each transaction, the data warehouse can be large and rich with potential insights. One can then mine the data (slice and dice) in many different ways and discover unique meaningful patterns. Aggregating the data helps improve the speed of analysis. A separate data warehouse allows analysis to go on separately in parallel, without burdening the operational database systems (Table 1.1).

Data Mining

Data Mining is the art and science of discovering useful innovative patterns from data. There is a wide variety of patterns that can be found in the data. There are many techniques, simple or complex, that help with finding patterns.

Table 1.1 Comparing database systems with data warehousing systems

Function	Database	Data Warehouse
Purpose	Data stored in databases can be used for many purposes including day-to-day operations	Data in data warehouse is cleansed data, which is useful for reporting and analysis
Granularity	Highly granular data including all activity and transaction details	Lower granularity data; rolled up to certain key dimensions of interest
Complexity	Highly complex with dozens or hundreds of data files, linked through common data fields	Typically organized around a large fact tables, and many lookup tables
Size	Database grows with growing volumes of activity and transactions. Old completed transactions are deleted to reduce size	Grows as data from operational databases is rolled up and appended every day. Data is retained for long-term trend analyses
Architectural choices	Relational, and object-oriented, databases	Star schema or Snowflake schema
Data access mechanisms	Primarily through high-level languages such as SQL. Traditional programming access database through Open Database Connectivity (ODBC) interfaces	Accessed through SQL; SQL output is forwarded to reporting tools and data visualization tools

In this example, a simple data analysis technique can be applied to the data in the data warehouse mentioned earlier. A simple cross-tabulation of results by quarter and products will reveal some easily visible patterns.

Movies Sales by Quarters—Cross-tabulation				
Qtr/Product	Gone With the Wind	Matrix	Monty Python	Total Sales
Q2	$15	0	$30	$45
Q3	$30	$36	$30	$96
Q4	$15	0	$18	$33
Total Sales	$60	$36	$78	$174

Based on this cross-tabulation, one can readily answer some product sales questions, such as:

1. What is the best selling movie by revenue?—***Monty Python***
2. What is the best quarter by revenue this year?—***Q3***
3. Any other patterns?—Matrix movie sells only in ***Q3 (seasonal item)***.

These simple insights can help plan marketing promotions and manage inventory of various movies.

If a cross-tabulation was designed to include customer location data, one could answer other questions, such as:

1. What is the best selling geography?—United States
2. What is the worst selling geography?—United Kingdom
3. Any other patterns?—Monty Python sells globally, while Gone with the Wind sells only in the United States.

If the data mining was done at the monthly level of data, it would be easy to miss the seasonality of the movies. However, one would have observed that September is the highest selling month.

The previous example shows that many differences and patterns can be noticed by analyzing data in different ways. However, some insights are more important than others. The value of the insight depends upon the problem being solved. The insight that there are more sales of a product in a certain quarter helps a manager plan what products to focus on. In this case, the store manager should stock up on Matrix in Quarter 3 (Q3). Similarly, knowing which quarter has the highest overall sales allows for different resource decisions in that quarter. In this case, if Q3 is bringing more than half of total sales, this requires greater attention on the e-commerce website in the third quarter.

Data mining should be done to solve high-priority, high-value problems. Much effort is required to gather data, clean and organize it, mine it with many techniques, interpret the results, and find the right insight. It is important that there be a large expected payoff from finding the insight. One should select the right data (and ignore the rest), organize it into a nice and imaginative framework that brings relevant data together, and then apply data mining techniques to deduce the right insight.

A retail company may use data mining techniques to determine which new product categories to add to which of their stores; how to increase sales of existing products; which new locations to open stores in; how to segment the customers for more effective communication; and so on.

Data can be analyzed at multiple levels of granularity and could lead to a large number of interesting combinations of data and interesting patterns. Some of the patterns may be more meaningful than the others. Such highly granular data is often used, especially in finance and high-tech areas, so that one can gain even the slightest edge over the competition.

Following are the brief descriptions of some of the most important data mining techniques used to generate insights from data.

Decision trees: They help classify populations into classes. It is said that 70 percent of all data mining work is about classification solutions; and that 70 percent of all classification work uses decision trees. Thus, decision trees are the most popular and important data mining technique. There are many popular algorithms to make decision trees. They differ in terms of their mechanisms and each technique work well for different situations. It is possible to try multiple algorithms on a data set and compare the predictive accuracy of each tree.

Regression: This is a well-understood technique from the field of statistics. The goal is to find a best fitting curve through the many data points. The best fitting curve is that which minimizes the (error) distance between the actual data points and the values predicted by the curve. Regression models can be projected into the future for prediction and forecasting purposes.

Artificial neural networks (ANNs): Originating in the field of artificial intelligence and machine learning, ANNs are multilayer nonlinear information processing models that learn from past data and predict future values. These models predict well, leading to their popularity. The model's parameters may not be very intuitive. Thus, neural networks are opaque like a black box. These systems also require a large amount of past data to adequately train the system.

Cluster analysis: This is an important data mining technique for dividing and conquering large data sets. The data set is divided into a certain number of clusters, by discerning similarities and dissimilarities within the data. There is no one right answer for the number of clusters in the data. The user needs to make a decision by looking at how well the number of clusters chosen fit the data. This is most commonly used for market segmentation. Unlike decision trees and regression, there is no one right answer for cluster analysis.

Association rule mining: Also called market basket analysis when used in retail industry, these techniques look for associations between data values. An analysis of items frequently found together in a market basket can help cross-sell products and also create product bundles.

Data Visualization

As data and insights grow in number, a new requirement is the ability of the executives and decision makers to absorb this information in real time. There is a limit to human comprehension and visualization capacity. That is a good reason to prioritize and manage with fewer but key variables that relate directly to the key result areas of a role.

Here are few considerations when presenting data:

1. Present the conclusions and not just report the data.
2. Choose wisely from a palette of graphs to suit the data.
3. Organize the results to make the central point stand out.
4. Ensure that the visuals accurately reflect the numbers. Inappropriate visuals can create misinterpretations and misunderstandings.
5. Make the presentation unique, imaginative, and memorable.

Executive dashboards are designed to provide information on select few variables for every executive. They use graphs, dials, and lists to show the status of important parameters. These dashboards also have a drill-down capability to enable a root-cause analysis of exceptional situations (Figure 1.3).

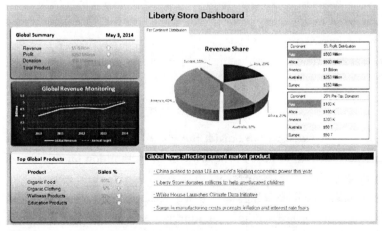

Figure 1.3 Sample executive dashboard

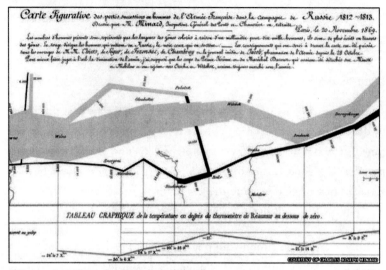

Figure 1.4 Sample data visualization

Data visualization has been an interesting problem across the disciplines. Many dimensions of data can be effectively displayed on a two-dimensional surface to give a rich and more insightful description of the totality of the story.

The classic presentation of the story of Napoleon's march to Russia in 1812, by French cartographer Joseph Minard, is shown in Figure 1.4. It covers about six dimensions. Time is on horizontal axis. The geographical coordinates and rivers are mapped in. The thickness of the bar shows the number of troops at any point of time that is mapped. One color is used for the onward march and another for the retreat. The weather temperature at each time is shown in the line graph at the bottom.

Organization of the Book

This chapter is designed to provide the wholeness of business intelligence and data mining, to provide the reader with an intuition for this area of knowledge. The rest of the book can be considered in three sections.

Section 1 will cover high-level topics. Chapter 2 will cover the field of business intelligence and its applications across industries and functions. Chapter 3 will briefly explain what data warehousing is and how it helps with data mining. Chapter 4 will then describe data mining in some detail with an overview of its major tools and techniques.

Section 2 is focused on data mining techniques. Every technique will be shown through solving an example in detail. Chapter 5 will show the power and ease of decision trees, which are the most popular data mining technique. Chapter 6 will describe statistical regression modeling techniques. Chapter 7 will provide an overview of ANNs. Chapter 8 will describe how cluster analysis can help with market segmentation. Finally, Chapter 9 will describe the association rule mining technique, also called market basket analysis, which helps find shopping patterns.

Section 3 will cover more advanced new topics. Chapter 10 will introduce the concepts and techniques of text mining, which helps discover insights from text data, including social media data. Chapter 11 will provide an overview of the growing field of web mining, which includes mining the structure, content, and usage of websites. Chapter 12 will provide an overview of the field of Big Data. Chapter 13 has been added as a primer on data modeling, for those who do not have any background in databases, and should be used if necessary.

Review Questions

1. Describe the business intelligence and data mining cycle.

2. Describe the data processing chain.

3. What are the similarities between diamond mining and data mining?

4. What are the different data mining techniques? Which of these would be relevant in your current work?

5. What is a dashboard? How does it help?

6. Create a visual to show the weather pattern in your city. Could you show together temperature, humidity, wind, and rain/snow over a period of time.

SECTION 1

This section covers three important high-level topics.

Chapter 2 will cover business intelligence concepts, and its applications in many industries.

Chapter 3 will describe data warehousing systems, and ways of creating and managing them.

Chapter 4 will describe data mining as a whole, with many do's and don'ts of effective data mining.

CHAPTER 2

Business Intelligence Concepts and Applications

Business intelligence (BI) is an umbrella term that includes a variety of IT applications that are used to analyze an organization's data and communicate the information to relevant users. Its major components are data warehousing, data mining, querying, and reporting (Figure 2.1).

The nature of life and businesses is to grow. Information is the life-blood of business. Businesses use many techniques for understanding their environment and predicting the future for their own benefit and growth. Decisions are made from facts and feelings. Data-based decisions are more effective than those based on feelings alone. Actions based on accurate data, information, knowledge, experimentation, and testing, using fresh insights, can more likely succeed and lead to sustained growth.

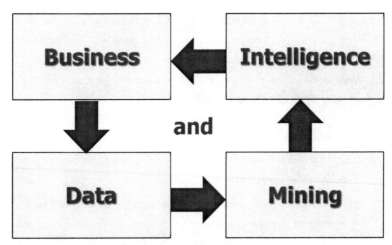

Figure 2.1 Business intelligence and data mining cycle

One's own data can be the most effective teacher. Therefore, organizations should gather data, sift through it, analyze and mine it, find insights, and then embed those insights into their operating procedures.

There is a new sense of importance and urgency around data as it is being viewed as a new natural resource. It can be mined for value, insights, and competitive advantage. In a hyperconnected world, where everything is potentially connected to everything else, with potentially infinite correlations, data represents the impulses of nature in the form of certain events and attributes. A skilled business person is motivated to use this cache of data to harness nature, and to find new niches of unserved opportunities that could become profitable ventures.

Caselet: Khan Academy—BI in Education

Khan Academy is an innovative nonprofit educational organization that is turning the K-12 education system upside down. It provides short You-Tube-based video lessons on thousands of topics for free. It shot into prominence when Bill Gates promoted it as a resource that he used to teach his own children. With this kind of a resource, classrooms are being flipped—that is, students do their basic lecture-type learning at home using those videos, while the class time is used for more one-on-one problem solving and coaching. Students can access the lessons at any time to learn at their own pace. The students' progress is recorded, including what videos they watched, how many times they watched, which problems they stumbled on, and what scores they got on online tests.

Khan Academy has developed tools to help teachers get a pulse on what is happening in the classroom. Teachers are provided a set of real-time dashboards to give them information from the macrolevel ("How is my class doing on geometry?") to the micro level ("How is Jane doing on mastering polygons?"). Armed with this information, teachers can place selective focus on the students that need certain help. (Source: KhanAcademy.org)

Q1. *How does a dashboard improve the teaching experience and the student's learning experience?*

Q2. *Design a dashboard for tracking your own career.*

BI for Better Decisions

The future is inherently uncertain. Risk is the result of a probabilistic world where there are no certainties and complexities abound. People use crystal balls, astrology, palmistry, ground hogs, and also mathematics and numbers to mitigate risk in decision-making. The goal is to make effective decisions, while reducing risk. Businesses calculate risks and make decisions based on a broad set of facts and insights. Reliable knowledge about the future can help managers make the right decisions with lower levels of risk.

The speed of action has risen exponentially with the growth of the Internet. In a hypercompetitive world, the speed of a decision and the consequent action can be a key advantage. The Internet and mobile technologies allow decisions to be made anytime, anywhere. Ignoring fast-moving changes can threaten the organization's future. Research has shown that an unfavorable comment about the company and its products on social media should not go unaddressed for long. Banks have had to pay huge penalties to Consumer Financial Protection Bureau (CFPB) in United States in 2013 for complaints made on CFPB's websites. On the other hand, a positive sentiment expressed on social media should also be utilized as a potential sales and promotion opportunity, while the opportunity lasts.

Decision Types

There are two main kinds of decisions: strategic decisions and operational decisions. BI can help make both better. Strategic decisions are those that impact the direction of the company. The decision to reach out to a new customer set would be a strategic decision. Operational decisions are more routine and tactical decisions, focused on developing greater efficiency. Updating an old website with new features will be an operational decision.

In strategic decision-making, the goal itself may or may not be clear, and the same is true for the path to reach the goal. The consequences of the decision would be apparent some time later. Thus, one is constantly scanning for new possibilities and new paths to achieve the goals. BI can help with what-if analysis of many possible scenarios. BI can also help create new ideas based on new patterns found from data mining.

Operational decisions can be made more efficient using an analysis of past data. A classification system can be created and modeled using the data of past instances to develop a good model of the domain. This model can help improve operational decisions in the future. BI can help automate operations level decision-making and improve efficiency by making millions of microlevel operational decisions in a model-driven way. For example, a bank might want to make decisions about making financial loans in a more scientific way using data-based models. A decision-tree-based model could provide a consistently accurate loan decisions. Developing such decision tree models is one of the main applications of data mining techniques.

Effective BI has an evolutionary component, as business models evolve. When people and organizations act, new facts (data) are generated. Current business models can be tested against the new data, and it is possible that those models will not hold up well. In that case, decision models should be revised and new insights should be incorporated. An unending process of generating fresh new insights in real time can help make better decisions, and thus can be a significant competitive advantage.

BI Tools

BI includes a variety of software tools and techniques to provide the managers with the information and insights needed to run the business. Information can be provided about the current state of affairs with the capability to drill down into details, and also insights about emerging patterns which lead to projections into the future. BI tools include data warehousing, online analytical processing, social media analytics, reporting, dashboards, querying, and data mining.

BI tools can range from very simple tools that could be considered end-user tools, to very sophisticated tools that offer a very broad and complex set of functionality. Thus, Even executives can be their own BI experts, or they can rely on BI specialists to set up the BI mechanisms for them. Thus, large organizations invest in expensive sophisticated BI solutions that provide good information in real time.

A spreadsheet tool, such as Microsoft Excel, can act as an easy but effective BI tool by itself. Data can be downloaded and stored in the spreadsheet, then analyzed to produce insights, then presented in the form of graphs and tables. This system offers limited automation using macros and other features. The analytical features include basic statistical and financial functions. Pivot tables help do sophisticated what-if analysis. Add-on modules can be installed to enable moderately sophisticated statistical analysis.

A dashboarding system, such as Tableau, can offer a sophisticated set of tools for gathering, analyzing, and presenting data. At the user end, modular dashboards can be designed and redesigned easily with a graphical user interface. The back-end data analytical capabilities include many statistical functions. The dashboards are linked to data warehouses at the back end to ensure that the tables and graphs and other elements of the dashboard are updated in real time (Figure 2.2).

Data mining systems, such as IBM SPSS Modeler, are industrial strength systems that provide capabilities to apply a wide range of analytical models on large data sets. Open source systems, such as Weka, are popular platforms designed to help mine large amounts of data to discover patterns.

Figure 2.2 Sample executive dashboard

BI Skills

As data grows and exceeds our capacity to make sense of it, the tools need to evolve, and so should the imagination of the BI specialist. "Data Scientist" has been called as the hottest job of this decade.

A skilled and experienced BI specialist should be open enough to go outside the box, open the aperture and see a wider perspective that includes more dimensions and variables, in order to find important patterns and insights. The problem needs to be looked at from a wider perspective to consider many more angles that may not be immediately obvious. An imaginative solution should be proposed for the problem so that interesting and useful results can emerge.

A good data mining project begins with an interesting problem to solve. Selecting the right data mining problem is an important skill. The problem should be valuable enough that solving it would be worth the time and expense. It takes a lot of time and energy to gather, organize, cleanse, and prepare the data for mining and other analysis. The data miner needs to persist with the exploration of patterns in the data. The skill level has to be deep enough to engage with the data and make it yield new useful insights.

BI Applications

BI tools are required in almost all industries and functions. The nature of the information and the speed of action may be different across businesses, but every manager today needs access to BI tools to have up-to-date metrics about business performance. Businesses need to embed new insights into their operating processes to ensure that their activities continue to evolve with more efficient practices. The following are some areas of applications of BI and data mining.

Customer Relationship Management

A business exists to serve a customer. A happy customer becomes a repeat customer. A business should understand the needs and sentiments of the customer, sell more of its offerings to the existing customers, and also, expand the pool of customers it serves. BI applications can impact many aspects of marketing.

1. *Maximize the return on marketing campaigns:* Understanding the customer's pain points from data-based analysis can ensure that the marketing messages are fine-tuned to better resonate with customers.

2. *Improve customer retention (churn analysis):* It is more difficult and expensive to win new customers than it is to retain existing customers. Scoring each customer on their likelihood to quit can help the business design effective interventions, such as discounts or free services, to retain profitable customers in a cost-effective manner.

3. *Maximize customer value (cross-selling, upselling):* Every contact with the customer should be seen as an opportunity to gauge their current needs. Offering a customer new products and solutions based on those imputed needs can help increase revenue per customer. Even a customer complaint can be seen as an opportunity to wow the customer. Using the knowledge of the customer's history and value, the business can choose to sell a premium service to the customer.

4. *Identify and delight highly valued customers:* By segmenting the customers, the best customers can be identified. They can be proactively contacted, and delighted, with greater attention and better service. Loyalty programs can be managed more effectively.

5. *Manage brand image:* A business can create a listening post to listen to social media chatter about itself. It can then do sentiment analysis of the text to understand the nature of comments and respond appropriately to the prospects and customers.

Health Care and Wellness

Health care is one of the biggest sectors in advanced economies. Evidence-based medicine is the newest trend in data-based health care management. BI applications can help apply the most effective diagnoses and prescriptions for various ailments. They can also help manage public health issues, and reduce waste and fraud.

1. *Diagnose disease in patients:* Diagnosing the cause of a medical condition is the critical first step in a medical engagement. Accurately diagnosing cases of cancer or diabetes can be a matter of life and death for the patient. In addition to the patient's own current situation, many

other factors can be considered, including the patient's health history, medication history, family's history, and other environmental factors. This makes diagnosis as much of an art form as it is science. Systems, such as IBM Watson, absorb all the medical research to date and make probabilistic diagnoses in the form of a decision tree, along with a full explanation for their recommendations. These systems take away most of the guess work done by doctors in diagnosing ailments.

2. *Treatment effectiveness:* The prescription of medication and treatment is also a difficult choice out of so many possibilities. For example, there are more than 100 medications for hypertension (high blood pressure) alone. There are also interactions in terms of which drugs work well with others and which drugs do not. Decision trees can help doctors learn about and prescribe more effective treatments. Thus, the patients could recover their health faster with a lower risk of complications and cost.

3. *Wellness management:* This includes keeping track of patient health records, analyzing customer health trends, and proactively advising them to take any needed precautions.

4. *Manage fraud and abuse:* Some medical practitioners have unfortunately been found to conduct unnecessary tests and/or overbill the government and health insurance companies. Exception-reporting systems can identify such providers, and action can be taken against them.

5. *Public health management:* The management of public health is one of the important responsibilities of any government. By using effective forecasting tools and techniques, governments can better predict the onset of disease in certain areas in real time. They can thus be better prepared to fight the diseases. Google has been known to predict the movement of certain diseases by tracking the search terms (like flu, vaccine) used in different parts of the world.

Education

As higher education becomes more expensive and competitive, it is a great user of data-based decision-making. There is a strong need for efficiency, increasing revenue, and improving the quality of student experience at all levels of education.

1. *Student enrolment (recruitment and retention):* Marketing to new potential students requires schools to develop profiles of the students that are most likely to attend. Schools can develop models of what kinds of students are attracted to the school, and then reach out to those students. The students at risk of not returning can be flagged, and corrective measures can be taken in time.

2. *Course offerings:* Schools can use the class enrolment data to develop models of which new courses are likely to be more popular with students. This can help increase class size, reduce costs, and improve student satisfaction.

3. *Alumni pledges:* Schools can develop predictive models of which alumni are most likely to pledge financial support to the school. Schools can create a profile for alumni more likely to pledge donations to the school. This could lead to a reduction in the cost of mailings and other forms of outreach to alumni.

Retail

Retail organizations grow by meeting customer needs with quality products, in a convenient, timely, and cost-effective manner. Understanding emerging customer shopping patterns can help retailers organize their products, inventory, store layout, and web presence in order to delight their customers, which in turn would help increase revenue and profits. Retailers generate a lot of transaction and logistics data that can be used to solve problems.

1. *Optimize inventory levels at different locations:* Retailers need to manage their inventories carefully. Carrying too much inventory imposes carrying costs, while carrying too little inventory can cause stock-outs and lost sales opportunities. Predicting sales trends dynamically can help retailers move inventory to where it is most in demand. Retail organizations can provide their suppliers with real-time information about sales of their items so that the suppliers can deliver their product to the right locations and minimize stock-outs.

2. *Improve store layout and sales promotions:* A market basket analysis can develop predictive models of which products sell together

often. This knowledge of affinities between products can help retailers co-locate those products. Alternatively, those affinity products could be located farther apart to make the customer walk the length and breadth of the store, and thus be exposed to other products. Promotional discounted product bundles can be created to push a nonselling item along with a set of products that sell well together.

3. *Optimize logistics for seasonal effects:* Seasonal products offer tremendously profitable short-term sales opportunities, yet they also offer the risk of unsold inventories at the end of the season. Understanding which products are in season in which market can help retailers dynamically manage prices to ensure their inventory is sold during the season. If it is raining in a certain area, then the inventory of umbrella and ponchos could be rapidly moved there from nonrainy areas to help increase sales.

4. *Minimize losses due to limited shelf life:* Perishable goods offer challenges in terms of disposing off the inventory in time. By tracking sales trends, the perishable products at risk of not selling before the sell-by date can be suitably discounted and promoted.

Banking

Banks make loans and offer credit cards to millions of customers. They are most interested in improving the quality of loans and reducing bad debts. They also want to retain more good customers and sell more services to them.

1. *Automate the loan application process:* Decision models can be generated from past data that predict the likelihood of a loan proving successful. These can be inserted in business processes to automate the financial loan application process.

2. *Detect fraudulent transactions:* Billions of financial transactions happen around the world every day. Exception-seeking models can identify patterns of fraudulent transactions. For example, if money is being transferred to an unrelated account for the first time, it could be a fraudulent transaction.

3. *Maximize customer value (cross-selling, upselling):* Selling more products and services to existing customers is often the easiest way to increase revenue. A checking account customer in good standing could be offered home, auto, or educational loans on more favorable terms than other customers, and thus, the value generated from that customer could be increased.

4. *Optimize cash reserves with forecasting:* Banks have to maintain certain liquidity to meet the needs of depositors who may like to withdraw money. Using past data and trend analysis, banks can forecast how much to keep, and invest the rest to earn interest.

Financial Services

Stock brokerages are an intensive user of BI systems. Fortunes can be made or lost based on access to accurate and timely information.

1. *Predict changes in bond and stock prices:* Forecasting the price of stocks and bonds is a favorite pastime of financial experts as well as lay people. Stock transaction data from the past, along with other variables, can be used to predict future price patterns. This can help traders develop long-term trading strategies.

2. *Assess the effect of events on market movements:* Decision models using decision trees can be created to assess the impact of events on changes in market volume and prices. Monetary policy changes (such as Fed Reserve interest rate change) or geopolitical changes (such as war in a part of the world) can be factored into the predictive model to help take action with greater confidence and less risk.

3. *Identify and prevent fraudulent activities in trading:* There have unfortunately been many cases of insider trading, leading to many prominent financial industry stalwarts going to jail. Fraud detection models can identify and flag fraudulent activity patterns.

Insurance

This industry is a prolific user of prediction models in pricing insurance proposals and managing losses from claims against insured assets.

1. *Forecast claim costs for better business planning:* When natural disasters, such as hurricanes and earthquakes, strike, loss of life and property occurs. By using the best available data to model the likelihood (or risk) of such events happening, the insurer can plan for losses and manage resources and profits effectively.

2. *Determine optimal rate plans:* Pricing an insurance rate plan requires covering the potential losses and making a profit. Insurers use actuary tables to project life spans and disease tables to project mortality rates, and thus price themselves competitively yet profitably.

3. *Optimize marketing to specific customers:* By microsegmenting potential customers, a data-savvy insurer can cherry-pick the best customers and leave the less profitable customers to its competitors. Progressive Insurance is a U.S.-based company that is known to actively use data mining to cherry-pick customers and increase its profitability.

4. *Identify and prevent fraudulent claim activities:* Patterns can be identified as to where and what kinds of fraud are more likely to occur. Decision-tree-based models can be used to identify and flag fraudulent claims.

Manufacturing

Manufacturing operations are complex systems with interrelated subsystems. From machines working right, to workers having the right skills, to the right components arriving with the right quality at the right time, to money to source the components, many things have to go right. Toyota's famous lean manufacturing company works on just-in-time inventory systems to optimize investments in inventory and to improve flexibility in their product mix.

1. *Discover novel patterns to improve product quality:* Quality of a product can also be tracked, and this data can be used to create a predictive model of product quality deteriorating. Many companies, such as automobile companies, have to recall their products if they have found defects that have a public safety implication. Data mining can help with root cause analysis that can be used to identify sources of errors and help improve product quality in the future.

2. *Predict/prevent machinery failures:* Statistically, all equipment is likely to break down at some point in time. Predicting which machine is likely to shut down is a complex process. Decision models to forecast machinery failures could be constructed using past data. Preventive maintenance can be planned, and manufacturing capacity can be adjusted, to account for such maintenance activities.

Telecom

BI in telecom can help with churn management, marketing/customer profiling, network failure, and fraud detection.

1. *Churn management:* Telecom customers have shown a tendency to switch their providers in search for better deals. Telecom companies tend to respond with many incentives and discounts to hold on to customers. However, they need to determine which customers are at a real risk of switching and which others are just negotiating for a better deal. The level of risk should to be factored into the kind of deals and discounts that should be given. Millions of such customer calls happen every month. The telecom companies need to provide a consistent and data-based way to predict the risk of the customer switching, and then make an operational decision in real time while the customer call is taking place. A decision-tree- or a neural network-based system can be used to guide the customer-service call operator to make the right decisions for the company, in a consistent manner.
2. *Marketing and product creation:* In addition to customer data, telecom companies also store call detail records (CDRs), which precisely describe the calling behavior of each customer. This unique data can be used to profile customers and then can be used for creating new products/services bundles for marketing purposes. An American telecom company, MCI, created a program called Friends & Family that allowed calls with one's friends and family on that network to be totally free and thus, effectively locked many people into their network.
3. *Network failure management:* Failure of telecom networks for technical failures or malicious attacks can have devastating impacts on

people, businesses, and society. In telecom infrastructure, some equipment will likely fail with certain mean time between failures. Modeling the failure pattern of various components of the network can help with preventive maintenance and capacity planning.

4. *Fraud management:* There are many kinds of fraud in consumer transactions. Subscription fraud occurs when a customer opens an account with the intention of never paying for the services. Superimposition fraud involves illegitimate activity by a person other than the legitimate account holder. Decision rules can be developed to analyze each CDR in real time to identify chances of fraud and take effective action.

Government

Government gathers a large amount of data by virtue of their regulatory function. That data could be analyzed for developing models of effective functioning.

1. *Law enforcement:* Social behavior is a lot more patterned and predictable than one would imagine. For example, Los Angeles Police Department (LAPD) mined the data from its 13 million crime records over 80 years and developed models of what kind of crime going to happen when and where. By increasing patrolling in those particular areas, LAPD was able to reduce property crime by 27 percent. Internet chatter can be analyzed to learn of and prevent any evil designs.

2. *Scientific research:* Any large collection of research data is amenable to being mined for patterns and insights. Protein folding (microbiology), nuclear reaction analysis (subatomic physics), disease control (public health) are some examples where data mining can yield powerful new insights.

Conclusion

BI is a comprehensive set of IT tools to support decision-making with imaginative solutions for a variety of problems. BI can help improve the performance in nearly all industries and applications.

Review Questions

1. Why should organizations invest in business intelligence solutions? Are these more important than IT security solutions? Why or why not?

2. List three business intelligence applications in the hospitality industry.

3. Describe two business intelligence tools used in your organization.

4. Businesses need a "two-second advantage" to succeed. What does that mean to you?

Liberty Stores Case Exercise: Step 1

Liberty Stores Inc is a specialized global retail chain that sells organic food, organic clothing, wellness products, and education products to enlightened LOHAS (Lifestyles of the Healthy and Sustainable) citizens worldwide. The company is 20 years old and is growing rapidly. It now operates in 5 continents, 50 countries, 150 cities, and has 500 stores. It sells 20,000 products and has 10,000 employees. The company has revenues of over $5 billion and has a profit of about 5 percent of revenue. The company pays special attention to the conditions under which the products are grown and produced. It donates about one-fifth (20 percent) of its pretax profits from global local charitable causes.

1. *Create a comprehensive dashboard for the CEO of the company.*
2. *Create another dashboard for a country head.*

CHAPTER 3

Data Warehousing

A data warehouse (DW) is an organized collection of integrated, subject-oriented databases designed to support decision support functions. DW is organized at the right level of granularity to provide clean enterprise-wide data in a standardized format for reports, queries, and analysis. DW is physically and functionally separate from an operational and transactional database. Creating a DW for analysis and queries represents significant investment in time and effort. It has to be constantly kept up-to-date for it to be useful. DW offers many business and technical benefits.

DW supports business reporting and data mining activities. It can facilitate distributed access to up-to-date business knowledge for departments and functions, thus improving business efficiency and customer service. DW can present a competitive advantage by facilitating decision making and helping reform business processes.

DW enables a consolidated view of corporate data, all cleaned and organized. Thus, the entire organization can see an integrated view of itself. DW thus provides better and timely information. It simplifies data access and allows end users to perform extensive analysis. It enhances overall IT performance by not burdening the operational databases used by Enterprise Resource Planning (ERP) and other systems.

Caselet: University Health System—BI in Health Care

Indiana University Health (IUH), a large academic health care system, decided to build an enterprise data warehouse (EDW) to foster a genuinely data-driven management culture. IUH hired a DW vendor to develop EDW, which also integrates with their electronic health record (EHR) system. They loaded 14 billion rows of data into EDW—fully 10 years of clinical data from across IUH's network. Clinical events, patient encounters, lab and radiology, and other patient data were included, as were IUH's performance management, revenue cycle, and patient satisfaction data. They soon put in a new interactive dashboard using the EDW that provided IUH's leadership with the daily operational insights they need to solve the quality/cost equation. It offers visibility into key operational metrics and trends to easily track the performance measures critical to controlling costs and maintaining quality. EDW can easily be used across IUH's departments to analyze, track, and measure clinical, financial, and patient experience outcomes. (Source: healthcatalyst.com)

    Q1. *What are the benefits of a single large comprehensive EDW?*

    Q1. *What kinds of data would be needed for EDW for an airline company?*

Design Considerations for DW

The objective of DW is to provide business knowledge to support decision making. For DW to serve its objective, it should be aligned around those decisions. It should be comprehensive, easy to access, and up-to-date. Here are some requirements for a good DW:

1. *Subject-oriented:* To be effective, DW should be designed around a subject domain, that is, to help solve a certain category of problems.
2. *Integrated:* DW should include data from many functions that can shed light on a particular subject area. Thus, the organization can benefit from a comprehensive view of the subject area.
3. *Time-variant (time series):* The data in DW should grow at daily or other chosen intervals. That allows latest comparisons over time.
4. *Nonvolatile:* DW should be persistent, that is, it should not be created on the fly from the operations databases. Thus, DW is consistently available for analysis, across the organization and over time.
5. *Summarized:* DW contains rolled-up data at the right level for queries and analysis. The rolling up helps create consistent granularity for effective comparisons. It helps reduces the number of variables or dimensions of the data to make them more meaningful for the decision makers.

6. *Not normalized:* DW often uses a star schema, which is a rectangular central table, surrounded by some lookup tables. The single-table view significantly enhances speed of queries.

7. *Metadata:* Many of the variables in the database are computed from other variables in the operational database. For example, total daily sales may be a computed field. The method of its calculation for each variable should be effectively documented. Every element in DW should be sufficiently well-defined.

8. *Near real-time and/or right-time (active):* DWs should be updated in near real-time in many high-transaction volume industries, such as airlines. The cost of implementing and updating DW in real time could discourage others. Another downside of real-time DW is the possibilities of inconsistencies in reports drawn just a few minutes apart.

DW Development Approaches

There are two fundamentally different approaches to developing DW: top down and bottom up. The top-down approach is to make a comprehensive DW that covers all the reporting needs of the enterprise. The bottom-up approach is to produce small data marts, for the reporting needs of different departments or functions, as needed. The smaller data marts will eventually align to deliver comprehensive EDW capabilities. The top-down approach provides consistency but takes time and resources. The bottom-up approach leads to healthy local ownership and maintainability of data (Table 3.1).

Table 3.1 Comparing data mart and data warehouse

	Functional Data Mart	Enterprise Data Warehouse
Scope	One subject or functional area	Complete enterprise data needs
Value	Functional area reporting and insights	Deeper insights connecting multiple functional areas
Target organization	Decentralized management	Centralized management
Time	Low to medium	High
Cost	Low	High
Size	Small to medium	Medium to large
Approach	Bottom up	Top down
Complexity	Low (fewer data transformations)	High (data standardization)
Technology	Smaller scale servers and databases	Industrial strength

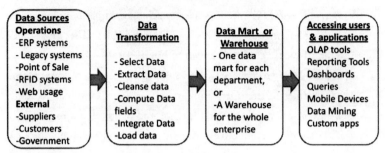

Figure 3.1 Data warehousing architecture

DW Architecture

DW has four key elements (Figure 3.1). The first element is the data sources that provide the raw data. The second element is the process of transforming that data to meet the decision needs. The third element is the methods of regularly and accurately loading of that data into EDW or data marts. The fourth element is the data access and analysis part, where devices and applications use the data from DW to deliver insights and other benefits to users.

Data Sources

DWs are created from structured data sources. Unstructured data, such as text data, would need to be structured before inserted into DW.

1. Operations data include data from all business applications, including from ERPs systems that form the backbone of an organization's IT systems. The data to be extracted will depend upon the subject matter of DW. For example, for a sales/marketing DW, only the data about customers, orders, customer service, and so on would be extracted.
2. Other applications, such as point-of-sale (POS) terminals and e-commerce applications, provide customer-facing data. Supplier data could come from supply chain management systems. Planning and budget data should also be added as needed for making comparisons against targets.
3. External syndicated data, such as weather or economic activity data, could also be added to DW, as needed, to provide good contextual information to decision makers.

Data Transformation Processes

The heart of a useful DW is the processes to populate the DW with good quality data. This is called the extract-transform-load (ETL) cycle.

1. Data should be extracted from many operational (transactional) database sources on a regular basis.
2. Extracted data should be aligned together by key fields. It should be cleansed of any irregularities or missing values. It should be rolled up together to the same level of granularity. Desired fields, such as daily sales totals, should be computed. The entire data should then be brought to the same format as the central table of DW.
3. The transformed data should then be uploaded into DW.

This ETL process should be run at a regular frequency. Daily transaction data can be extracted from ERPs, transformed, and uploaded to the database the same night. Thus, DW is up-to-date next morning. If DW is needed for near-real-time information access, then the ETL processes would need to be executed more frequently. ETL work is usually automated using programing scripts that are written, tested, and then deployed for periodic updating DW.

DW Design

Star schema is the preferred data architecture for most DWs. There is a central fact table that provides most of the information of interest. There are lookup tables that provide detailed values for codes used in the central table. For example, the central table may use digits to represent a sales person. The lookup table will help provide the name for that sales person code. Here is an example of a star schema for a data mart for monitoring sales performance (Figure 3.2).

Other schemas include the snowflake architecture. The difference between a star and snowflake is that in the latter, the lookup tables can have their own further lookup tables.

There are many technology choices for developing DW. This includes selecting the right database management system and the right set of data management tools. There are a few big and reliable providers of DW systems. The provider of the operational DBMS may be chosen for DW also.

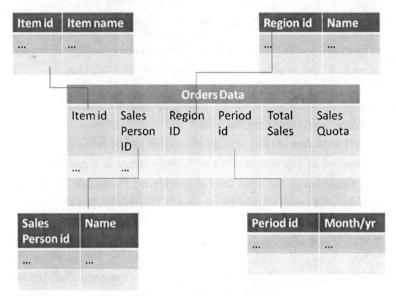

Figure 3.2 Star schema architecture

Alternatively, a best-of-breed DW vendor could be used. There are also a variety of tools out there for data migration, data upload, data retrieval, and data analysis.

DW Access

Data from DW could be accessed for many purposes, through many devices.

1. A primary use of DW is to produce routine management and monitoring reports. For example, a sales performance report would show sales by many dimensions, and compared with plan. A dashboarding system will use data from the warehouse and present analysis to users. The data from DW can be used to populate customized performance dashboards for executives. The dashboard could include drill-down capabilities to analyze the performance data for root cause analysis.
2. The data from the warehouse could be used for ad hoc queries and any other applications that make use of the internal data.

3. Data from DW is used to provide data for mining purposes. Parts of the data would be extracted, and then combined with other relevant data, for data mining.

DW Best Practices

A DW project reflects a significant investment into IT. All of the best practices in implementing any IT project should be followed.

1. The DW project should align with the corporate strategy. Top management should be consulted for setting objectives. Financial viability Return on Investment (ROI) should be established. The project must be managed by both IT and business professionals. The DW design should be carefully tested before beginning development work. It is often much more expensive to redesign after development work has begun.
2. It is important to manage user expectations. DW should be built incrementally. Users should be trained in using the system, and absorb the many features of the system.
3. Quality and adaptability should be built in from the start. Only cleansed and high-quality data should be loaded. The system should be able to adapt to new access tools. As business needs change, new data marts can be created for new needs.

Conclusion

DWs are special data management facilities intended for creating reports and analysis to support managerial decision making. They are designed to make reporting and querying simple and efficient. The sources of data are operational systems and external data sources. DW needs to be updated with new data regularly to keep it useful. Data from DW provides a useful input for data mining activities.

Review Questions

1. What is the purpose of a data warehouse?
2. What are the key elements of a data warehouse? Describe each.

3. What are the sources and types of data for a data warehouse?
4. How will data warehousing evolve in the age of social media?

Liberty Stores Case Exercise: Step 2

The Liberty Stores company wants to be fully informed about its sales of products and take advantage of growth opportunities as they arise. It wants to analyze sales of all its products by all store locations. The newly hired chief knowledge officer has decided to build a data warehouse.

1. *Design a DW structure for the company to monitor its sales performance. (Hint: Design the central table and lookup tables.)*
2. *Design another DW for the company's sustainability and charitable activities.*

CHAPTER 4

Data Mining

Data mining is the art and science of discovering knowledge, insights, and patterns in data. It is the act of extracting useful patterns from an organized collection of data. Patterns must be valid, novel, potentially useful, and understandable. The implicit assumption is that data about the past can reveal patterns of activity that can be projected into the future.

Data mining is a multidisciplinary field that borrows techniques from a variety of fields. It utilizes the knowledge of data quality and data organizing from the databases area. It draws modeling and analytical techniques from statistics and computer science (artificial intelligence) areas. It also draws the knowledge of decision-making from the field of business management.

The field of data mining emerged in the context of pattern recognition in defense, such as identifying a friend-or-foe on a battlefield. Like many other defense-inspired technologies, it has evolved to help gain a competitive advantage in business.

For example, "customers who buy *cheese* and *milk* also buy *bread* 90 percent of the time" would be a useful pattern for a grocery store, which can then stock the products appropriately. Similarly, "people with blood pressure greater than 160 and an age greater than 65 were at a high risk of dying from a heart stroke" is of great diagnostic value for doctors, who can then focus on treating such patients with urgent care and great sensitivity.

Past data can be of predictive value in many complex situations, especially where the pattern may not be so easily visible without the modeling technique. Here is a dramatic case of a data-driven decision-making system that beats the best of human experts. Using past data, a decision tree model was developed to predict votes for Justice Sandra Day O'Connor, who had a swing vote in a 5–4 divided US Supreme Court. All her previous decisions were coded on a few variables. What emerged from data mining was a simple four-step decision tree that was able to accurately predict her votes

71 percent of the time. In contrast, the legal analysts could at best predict correctly 59 percent of the time. *(Source: Martin et al. 2004)*

Caselet: Target Corp—Data Mining in Retail

Target is a large retail chain that crunches data to develop insights that help target marketing and advertising campaigns. Target analysts managed to develop a pregnancy-prediction score based on a customer's purchasing history of 25 products. In a widely publicized story, they figured out that a teenage girl was pregnant before her father did. The targeting can be quite successful and dramatic as this example published in the New York Times illustrates as follows:

About a year after Target created their pregnancy-prediction model, a man walked into a Target store and demanded to see the manager. He was clutching coupons that had been sent to his daughter and he was angry, according to an employee who participated in the conversation. "My daughter got this in the mail!" he said. "She's still in high school, and you're sending her coupons for baby clothes and cribs? Are you trying to encourage her to get pregnant?"

The manager didn't have any idea what the man was talking about. He looked at the mailer. Sure enough, it was addressed to the man's daughter and contained advertisements for maternity clothing, nursery furniture and pictures of smiling infants. The manager apologized and then called a few days later to apologize again.

On the phone, though, the father was somewhat subdued. "I had a talk with my daughter," he said. "It turns out there's been some activities in my house I haven't been completely aware of. I owe you an apology." (Source: New York Times)

Q1. *Do Target and other retailers have full rights to use their acquired data as it sees fit, and to contact desired consumers with all legally admissible means and messages? What are the issues involved here?*

Q2. *FaceBook and Google provide many services for free. In return they mine our email and blogs and send us targeted ads. Is that a fair deal?*

Gathering and Selecting Data

The total amount of data in the world is doubling every 18 months. There is an ever-growing avalanche of data coming with higher velocity, volume, and variety. One has to quickly use it or lose it. Smart data mining requires choosing where to play. One has to make judicious decisions about what to gather and what to ignore, based on the purpose of the data mining exercises. It is like deciding where to fish; not all streams of data will be equally rich in potential insights.

To learn from data, one needs to effectively gather quality data, clean and organize it, and then efficiently process it. One requires the skills and technologies for consolidation and integration of data elements from many sources. Most organizations develop an enterprise data model (EDM), which is a unified, high-level model of all the data stored in an organization's databases. The EDM will be inclusive of the data generated from all internal systems. The EDM provides the basic menu of data to create a data warehouse for a particular decision-making purpose. Data warehouses help organize all this data in a useful manner so that it can be selected and deployed for mining. The EDM can also help imagine what relevant external data should be gathered to develop good predictive relationships with the internal data. In the United States, the governments and their agencies make a vast variety and quantity of data available at data.gov.

Gathering and curating data takes time and effort, particularly when it is unstructured or semistructured. Unstructured data can come in many forms like databases, blogs, images, videos, and chats. There are streams of unstructured social media data from blogs, chats, and tweets. There are also streams of machine-generated data from connected machines, RFID tags, the internet of things, and so on. The data should be put in rectangular data shapes with clear columns and rows before submitting it to data mining.

Knowledge of the business domain helps select the right streams of data for pursuing new insights. Data that suits the nature of the problem being solved should be gathered. The data elements should be relevant, and suitably address the problem being solved. They could directly impact the problem, or they could be a suitable proxy for the effect being measured. Select data will also be gathered from the data warehouse.

Industries and functions will have their own requirements and con-straints. The health care industry will provide a different type of data with different data names. The HR function would provide different kinds of data. There would be different issues of quality and privacy for these data.

Data Cleansing and Preparation

The quality of data is critical to the success and value of the data mining project. Otherwise, the situation will be of the kind of garbage in and garbage out (GIGO). The quality of incoming data varies by the source and nature of data. Data from internal operations is likely to be of higher quality, as it will be accurate and consistent. Data from social media and other public sources is less under the control of business, and is less likely to be reliable.

Data almost certainly needs to be cleansed and transformed before it can be used for data mining. There are many ways in what data may need to be cleansed—filling missing values, reigning in the effects of outliers, transforming fields, binning continuous variables, and much more—before it can be ready for analysis. Data cleansing and preparation is a labor-intensive or semiautomated activity that can take up to 60 to 70 percent of the time needed for a data mining project.

1. Duplicate data needs to be removed. The same data may be received from multiple sources. When merging the data sets, data must be de-duped.

2. Missing values need to be filled in, or those rows should be removed from analysis. Missing values can be filled in with average or modal or default values.

3. Data elements may need to be transformed from one unit to an-other. For example, total costs of health care and the total number of patients may need to be reduced to cost/patient to allow comparabil-ity of that value.

4. Continuous values may need to be binned into a few buckets to help with some analyses. For example, work experience could be binned as low, medium, and high.

5. Data elements may need to be adjusted to make them comparable over time. For example, currency values may need to be adjusted

for inflation; they would need to be converted to the same base year for comparability. They may need to be converted to a common currency.

6. Outlier data elements need to be removed after careful review, to avoid the skewing of results. For example, one big donor could skew the analysis of alumni donors in an educational setting.

7. Any biases in the selection of data should be corrected to ensure the data is representative of the phenomena under analysis. If the data includes many more members of one gender than is typical of the population of interest, then adjustments need to be applied to the data.

8. Data should be brought to the same granularity to ensure comparability. Sales data may be available daily, but the sales person compensation data may only be available monthly. To relate these variables, the data must be brought to the lowest common denominator, in this case, monthly.

9. Data may need to be selected to increase information density. Some data may not show much variability, because it was not properly recorded or for any other reasons. This data may dull the effects of other differences in the data and should be removed to improve the information density of the data.

Outputs of Data Mining

Data mining techniques can serve different types of objectives. The outputs of data mining will reflect the objective being served. There are many representations of the outputs of data mining.

One popular form of data mining output is a decision tree. It is a hierarchically branched structure that helps visually follow the steps to make a model-based decision. The tree may have certain attributes, such as probabilities assigned to each branch. A related format is a set of business rules, which are if-then statements that show causality. A decision tree can be mapped to business rules. If the objective function is prediction, then a decision tree or business rules are the most appropriate mode of representing the output.

The output can be in the form of a regression equation or mathematical function that represents the best fitting curve to represent the data. This equation may include linear and nonlinear terms. Regression equations are a good way of representing the output of classification exercises. These are also a good representation of forecasting formulae.

Population "centroid" is a statistical measure for describing central tendencies of a collection of data points. These might be defined in a multidimensional space. For example, a centroid could be "middle-aged, highly educated, high-net worth professionals, married with two children, living in the coastal areas". Or a population of "20-something, ivy-league-educated, tech entrepreneurs based in Silicon Valley". Or a collection of "vehicles more than 20 years old, giving low mileage per gallon, which failed the environmental inspection". These are typical representations of the output of a cluster analysis exercise.

Business rules are an appropriate representation of the output of a market basket analysis exercise. These rules are if-then statements with some probability parameters associated with each rule. For example, those that buy milk and bread will also buy butter (with 80 percent probability).

Evaluating Data Mining Results

There are two primary kinds of data mining processes: supervised learning and unsupervised learning. In supervised learning, a decision model can be created using past data, and the model can then be used to predict the correct answer for future data instances. Classification is the main category of supervised learning activity. There are many techniques for classification, decision trees being the most popular one. Each of these techniques can be implemented with many algorithms. A common metric for all of classification techniques is predictive accuracy.

Predictive Accuracy = (Correct Predictions) / Total Predictions

Suppose a data mining project has been initiated to develop a predictive model for cancer patients using a decision tree. Using a relevant set of variables and data instances, a decision tree model has been created. The model is then used to predict other data instances. When a true positive data point is positive, that is a correct prediction, called a true positive (TP). Similarly, when a true negative data point is classified as negative, that is a true negative (TN). On the other hand, when a true-positive data

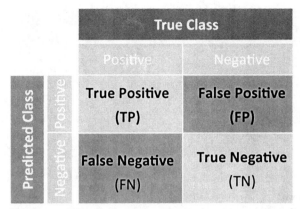

Figure 4.1 Confusion matrix

point is classified by the model as negative, that is an incorrect prediction, called a false negative (FN). Similarly, when a true-negative data point is classified as positive, that is classified as a false positive (FP). This is called the confusion matrix (Figure 4.1).

Thus, the predictive accuracy can be specified by the following formula.

Predictive Accuracy = (TP + TN) / (TP + TN + FP + FN).

All classification techniques have a predictive accuracy associated with a predictive model. The highest value can be 100 percent. In practice, predictive models with more than 70 percent accuracy can be considered usable in business domains, depending upon the nature of the business.

There are no good objective measures to judge the accuracy of unsupervised learning techniques, such as cluster analysis. There is no single right answer for the results of these techniques. The value of the segmentation model depends upon the value the decision maker sees in those results.

Data Mining Techniques

Data may be mined to help make more efficient decisions in the future. Or it may be used to explore the data to find interesting associative patterns. The right technique depends upon the kind of problem being solved (Figure 4.2).

Important Data Mining Techniques		
Supervised Learning: Classification	Machine Learning Techniques	Decision Trees
		Artificial Neural Networks
	Statistical Techniques	Regression
Unsupervised Learning: Exploration	Machine Learning Techniques	Cluster Analysis
		Association Rule Mining

Figure 4.2 Important data mining techniques

The most important class of problems solved using data mining are classification problems. These are problems where data from past decisions is mined to extract the few rules and patterns that would improve the accuracy of the decision-making process in the future. The data of past decisions is organized and mined for decision rules or equations, which are then codified to produce more accurate decisions. Classification techniques are called supervised learning as there is a way to supervise whether the model's prediction is right or wrong.

A decision tree is a hierarchically organized branched, structured to help make decision in an easy and logical manner. *Decision trees* are the most popular data mining technique, for many reasons.

1. Decision trees are easy to understand and easy to use, by analysts as well as executives. They also show a high predictive accuracy.
2. They select the most relevant variables automatically out of all the available variables for decision-making.
3. Decision trees are tolerant of data quality issues and do not require much data preparation from the users.
4. Even nonlinear relationships can be handled well by decision trees.

There are many algorithms to implement decision trees. Some of the popular ones are C5, CART, and CHAID.

Regression is a relatively simple and the most popular statistical data mining technique. The goal is to fit a smooth well-defined curve to the data. Regression analysis techniques, for example, can be used to model and predict the energy consumption as a function of daily temperature. Simply plotting the data shows a nonlinear curve. Applying a nonlinear regression equation will fit the data very well with high accuracy. Thus, the energy consumption on any future day can be predicted using this equation.

Artificial neural network (ANN) is a sophisticated data mining technique from the Artificial Intelligence stream in Computer Science. It mimics the behavior of human neural structure: Neurons receive stimuli, process them, and communicate their results to other neurons successively, and eventually a neuron outputs a decision. A decision task may be processed by just one neuron and the result may be communicated soon. Alternatively, there could be many layers of neurons involved in a decision task, depending upon the complexity of the domain. The neural network can be trained by making a decision over and over again with many data points. It will continue to learn by adjusting its internal computation and communication parameters based on feedback received on its previous decisions. The intermediate values passed within the layers of neurons may not make intuitive sense to an observer. Thus, the neural networks are considered a black-box system.

At some point, the neural network will have learned enough and begin to match the predictive accuracy of a human expert or alternative classification techniques. The predictions of some ANNs that have been trained over a long period of time with a large amount of data have become decisively more accurate than human experts. At that point, the ANNs can begin to be seriously considered for deployment, in real situations in real time.

ANNs are popular because they are eventually able to reach a high predictive accuracy. ANNs are also relatively simple to implement and do not have any issues with data quality. ANNs require a lot of data to train to develop good predictive ability.

Cluster analysis is an exploratory learning technique that helps in identifying a set of similar groups in the data. It is a technique used for automatic identification of natural groupings of things. Data instances that are similar to (or near) each other are categorized into one cluster, while data instances that are very different (or far away) from each other are categorized into separate clusters. There can be any number of clusters that could be produced by the data. The K-means technique is a popular technique and allows the user guidance in selecting the right number (K) of clusters from the data.

Clustering is also known as the segmentation technique. The technique shows the clusters of things from past data. The output is the centroids for each cluster and the allocation of data points to their cluster. The centroid definition is used to assign new data instances that can be assigned to their cluster homes. Clustering is also a part of the artificial intelligence family of techniques.

Association rules are a popular data mining method in business, especially where selling is involved. Also known as market basket analysis, it helps in answering questions about cross-selling opportunities. This is the heart of the personalization engine used by e-commerce sites like Amazon.com and streaming movie sites like Netflix.com. The technique helps find interesting relationships (affinities) between variables (items or events). These are represented as rules of the form $X \Rightarrow Y$, where X and Y are sets of data items. A form of unsupervised learning, it has no dependent variable; and there are no right or wrong answers. There are just stronger and weaker affinities. Thus, each rule has a confidence level assigned to it. A part of the machine-learning family, this technique achieved legendary status when a fascinating relationship was found in the sales of diapers and beers.

Tools and Platforms for Data Mining

Data mining tools have existed for many decades. However, they have recently become more important as the values of data have grown and the field of big data analytics has come into prominence. There are a wide range of data mining platforms available in the market today.

1. There are simple end-user data mining tools, such as MS Excel, and there are more sophisticated tools, such as IBM SPSS Modeler.
2. There are stand-alone tools, and there are tools embedded in an existing transaction processing or data warehousing or ERP system.
3. There are open-source and freely available tools, such as Weka, and there are commercial products.

4. There are text-based tools that require some programing skills, and there are Graphical User Interface (GUI)-based drag-and-drop format tools.
5. There are tools that work only on proprietary data formats, and there are those directly accept data from a host of popular data management tools formats.

Here, we compare three platforms that we have used extensively and effectively for many data mining projects (Table 4.1).

MS Excel is a relatively simple and easy data mining tool. It can get quite versatile once analyst pack and some other add-on products are installed on it.

IBM's SPSS Modeler is an industry-leading data mining platform. It offers a powerful set of tools and algorithms for most popular data mining capabilities. It has colorful GUI format with drag-and-drop capabilities. It can accept data in multiple formats, including reading Excel files directly.

Weka is an open-source GUI-based tool that offers a large number of data mining algorithms.

ERP systems include some data analytic capabilities, too. SAP has its Business Objects BI software. Business Objects is considered one of the leading BI suites in the industry and is often used by organizations that use SAP.

Table 4.1 Comparison of popular data mining platforms

Feature	Excel	IBM SPSS Modeler	Weka
Ownership	Commercial	Commercial, expensive	Open-source, free
Data mining features	Limited, extensible with add-on modules	Extensive features, unlimited data sizes	Extensive, performance issues with large data
Stand-alone	Stand-alone	Embedded in BI software suites	Stand-alone
User skills needed	End users	Skilled BI analysts	Skilled BI analysts
User interface	Select and click, easy	Drag-and-drop use, colorful, beautiful GUI	GUI, mostly b&w text output
Data formats	Industry standard	Variety of data sources accepted	Proprietary

Data Mining Best Practices

Effective and successful use of data mining activity requires both business and technology skills. The business aspects help understand the domain and the key questions. It also helps one imagine possible relationships in the data and create hypotheses to test it. The IT aspects help fetch the data from many sources, clean up the data, assemble it to meet the needs of the business problem, and then run the data mining techniques on the platform.

An important element is to go after the problem iteratively. It is better to divide and conquer the problem with smaller amounts of data, and get closer to the heart of the solution in an iterative sequence of steps. There are several best practices learned from the use of data mining techniques over a long period of time. The data mining industry has proposed a Cross-Industry Standard Process for Data Mining (CRISP-DM). It has six essential steps (Figure 4.3):

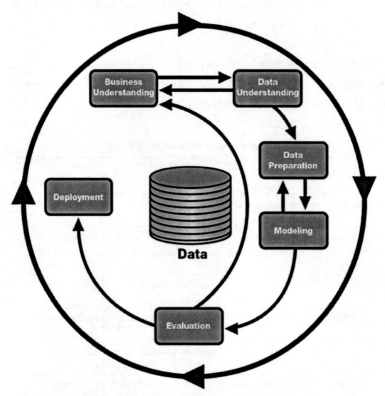

Figure 4.3 CRISP-DM data mining cycle

1. The first and most important step in data mining is business under-standing, that is, asking the right business questions. A question is a good one if answering it would lead to large payoffs for the organization, financially and otherwise. In other words, selecting a data mining project is like any other project, in which it should show strong payoffs if the project is successful. There should be strong executive support for the data mining project, which means that the project aligns well with the business strategy.

2. A second important step is to be creative and open in proposing imaginative hypotheses for the solution. Thinking outside the box is important, both in terms of a proposed model as well in the data sets available and required.

3. The data should be clean and of high quality. It is important to assemble a team that has a mix of technical and business skills, who understand the domain and the data. Data cleaning can take 60 to 70 percent of the time in a data mining project. It may be desirable to add new data elements from external sources of data that could help improve predictive accuracy.

4. Patience is required in continuously engaging with the data until the data yields some good insights. A host of modeling tools and algorithms should be used. A tool could be tried with different options, such as running different decision tree algorithms.

5. One should not accept what the data says at first. It is better to triangulate the analysis by applying multiple data mining techniques and conducting many what-if scenarios, to build confidence in the solution. Evaluate the model's predictive accuracy with more test data.

6. The dissemination and rollout of the solution is the key to project success. Otherwise the project will be a waste of time and will be a setback for establishing and supporting a data-based decision-process culture in the organization. The model should be embedded in the organization's business processes.

Myths about Data Mining

There are many myths about this area, scaring away many business executives from using data mining.

Myth #1: Data mining is about algorithms: Data mining is used by business to answer important and practical business questions. Formulating the problem statement correctly and identifying imaginative solutions for testing are far more important before the data mining algorithms get called in.

Myth #2: Data mining is about predictive accuracy: While important, predictive accuracy is a feature of the algorithm. As in myth #1, the quality of output is a strong function of the right problem, right hypothesis, and the right data.

Myth #3: Data mining requires a data warehouse: While the presence of a data warehouse assists in the gathering of information, sometimes the creation of the data warehouse itself can benefit from some exploratory data mining.

Myth #4: Data mining requires large quantities of data: Many interesting data mining exercises are done using small- or medium-sized data sets.

Myth #5: Data mining requires a technology expert: Many interesting data mining exercises are done by end users and executives using simple everyday tools like spreadsheets.

Data Mining Mistakes

Data mining is an exercise in extracting nontrivial useful patterns in the data. It requires a lot of preparation and patience to pursue the many leads that data may provide. Much domain knowledge, tools, and skill are required to find such patterns. Here are some of the more common mistakes in doing data mining, and should be avoided.

Mistake #1: Selecting the wrong problem for data mining: Without the right goals or having no goals, data mining leads to a waste of time. Getting the right answer to an irrelevant question could be interesting, but it would be pointless.

Mistake #2: Buried under mountains of data without clear metadata: It is more important to be engaged with the data, than to have lots of data. The relevant data required may be much less than initially thought. There may be insufficient knowledge about the data or metadata.

Mistake #3: Disorganized data mining: Without clear goals, much time is wasted. Doing the same tests using the same mining algorithms repeatedly and blindly, without thinking about the next stage, without a plan, would lead to wasted time and energy. This can come from being sloppy about keeping track of the data mining procedure and results.

Mistake #4: Insufficient business knowledge: Without a deep understanding of the business domain, the results would be gibberish and meaningless. Do not make erroneous assumptions, courtesy of experts. Do not rule out anything when observing data analysis results. Do not ignore suspicious (good or bad) findings and quickly move on. Be open to surprises. Even when insights emerge at one level, it is important to sliced and dice the data at other levels to see if more powerful insights can be extracted.

Mistake #5: Incompatibility of data mining tools: All the tools from data gathering, preparation, mining, and visualization should work together.

Mistake #6: Locked in the data jailhouse: Use tools that can work with data from multiple sources in multiple industry standard formats.

Mistake #7: Looking only at aggregated results and not at individual records/predictions. It is possible that the right results at the aggregate level provide absurd conclusions at an individual record level.

Mistake #8: Running out of time: Not leaving sufficient time for data acquisition, selection, and preparation can lead to data quality issues and GIGO. Similarly not providing enough time for testing the model, training the users and deploying the system can make the project a failure.

Mistake #9: Measuring your results differently from the way your sponsor measures them: This comes from losing a sense of business objectives and beginning to mine data for its own sake.

Mistake #10: Naively believing everything you are told about the data: Also naively believing everything you are told about your own data mining analysis.

Conclusion

Data mining is like diving into the rough material to discover a valuable finished nugget. While the technique is important, domain knowledge is also important to provide imaginative solutions that can then be tested with data mining. The business objective should be well understood and should always be kept in mind to ensure that the results are beneficial to the sponsor of the exercise.

Review Questions

1. What is data mining? What are supervised and unsupervised learning techniques?
2. Describe the key steps in the data mining process. Why is it important to follow these processes?
3. What is a confusion matrix?
4. Why is data preparation so important and time consuming?
5. What are some of the most popular data mining techniques?
6. What are the major mistakes to be avoided when doing data mining?
7. What are the key requirements for a skilled data analyst?

Liberty Stores Case Exercise: Step 3

Liberty is constantly evaluating opportunities for improving efficiencies in all its operations, including the commercial operations as well its charitable activities.

1. *What data mining techniques would you use to analyze and predict sales patterns?*
2. *What data mining technique would you use to categorize its customers?*

SECTION 2

This section will cover the most important data mining techniques in detail. The first three techniques are examples of supervised learning, consisting of classification techniques.

Chapter 5 will cover decision trees, which are the most popular form of data mining techniques. There are many algorithms to develop decision trees.

Chapter 6 will describe regression modeling techniques. These are statistical techniques.

Chapter 7 will cover artificial neural networks.

The next two techniques are examples of unsupervised learning, consisting of data exploration techniques.

Chapter 8 will cover cluster analysis. This is also called market segmentation analysis.

Chapter 9 will cover the association rule mining technique, also called market basket analysis.

CHAPTER 5

Decision Trees

Decision trees are a simple way to guide one's path to a decision. The decision may be a simple binary one, whether to approve a loan or not. Or it may be a complex multivalued decision, as to what may be the diagnosis for a particular sickness. Decision trees are hierarchically branched structures that help one come to a decision based on asking certain questions in a particular sequence. Decision trees are one of the most widely used techniques for classification. A good decision tree should be short and ask only a few meaningful questions. They are very efficient to use, easy to explain, and their classification accuracy is competitive with other methods. Decision trees can generate knowledge from a few test instances that can then be applied to a broad population. Decision trees are used mostly to answer relatively simple binary decisions.

Caselet: Predicting Heart Attacks Using Decision Trees

A study was done at UC San Diego concerning heart disease patient data. The patients were diagnosed with a heart attack from chest pain, diagnosed by EKG, high enzyme levels in their heart muscles, and so on. The objective was to predict which of these patients was at risk of dying from a second heart attack within the next 30 days. The prediction would determine the treatment plan, such as whether to keep the patient in intensive care or not. For each patient, more than 100 variables were collected, including demographics, medical history, and lab data. Using that data and the CART algorithm, a decision tree was constructed.

The decision tree showed that if blood pressure (BP) was low (≤90), the chance of another heart attack was very high (70 percent). If the patient's BP was OK, the next question to ask was the patient's age. If the age was low (≤62), then the patient's survival was almost guaranteed (98 percent). If the age was higher, then the next question to ask was about sinus problems. If their sinus was OK, the chances of survival were 89 percent. Otherwise, the chance of survival dropped to 50 percent. This decision tree predicts 86.5 percent of the cases correctly. (Source: Salford Systems)

> Q1. *Is a decision tree good enough in terms of accuracy, design, readability, for this data, and so on?*
>
> Q2. *Identify the benefits from creating such a decision tree. Can these be quantified?*

Decision Tree Problem

Imagine a conversation between a doctor and a patient. The doctor asks questions to determine the cause of the ailment. The doctor would continue to ask questions, till he or she is able to arrive at a reasonable decision. If nothing seems plausible, he or she might recommend some tests to generate more data and options.

This is how experts in any field solve problems. They use decision trees or decision rules. For every question they ask, the potential answers create separate branches for further questioning. For each branch, the expert would know how to proceed ahead. The process continues until the end of the tree is reached, which means a leaf node is reached.

Human experts learn from past experiences or data points. Similarly, a machine can be trained to learn from the past data points and extract some knowledge or rules from it. Decision trees use machine-learning algorithms to abstract knowledge from data. A decision tree would have a predictive accuracy based on how often it makes correct decisions.

1. The more training data is provided, the more accurate its knowledge extraction will be, and thus, it will make more accurate decisions.
2. The more variables the tree can choose from, the tree will come out better with higher accuracy.
3. In addition, a good decision tree should also be frugal so that it takes the least number of questions, and thus, the least amount of effort, to get to the right decision.

Here is an exercise to create a decision tree that helps make decisions about approving the play of an outdoor game. The objective is to predict the *play* decision given the atmospheric conditions out there. The decision is: Should the game be allowed or not? Here is the decision problem.

Outlook	Temp	Humidity	Windy	Play
Sunny	Hot	Normal	True	?

To answer that question, one should look at past experience and see what decision was made in a similar instance, if such an instance exists. One could look up the database of past decisions to find the answer and try to come to an answer. Here is a list of the decisions taken in 14 instances of past soccer game situations (Dataset courtesy: Witten, Frank, and Hall 2010).

Outlook	Temp	Humidity	Windy	Play
Sunny	Hot	High	False	No
Sunny	Hot	High	True	No
Overcast	Hot	High	False	Yes
Rainy	Mild	High	False	Yes
Rainy	Cool	Normal	False	Yes
Rainy	Cool	Normal	True	No
Overcast	Cool	Normal	True	Yes
Sunny	Mild	High	False	No
Sunny	Cool	Normal	False	Yes
Rainy	Mild	Normal	False	Yes
Sunny	Mild	Normal	True	Yes
Overcast	Mild	High	True	Yes
Overcast	Hot	Normal	False	Yes
Rainy	Mild	High	True	No

If there were a row for *sunny/hot/normal/windy* condition in the data table, it would match the current problem, and the decision from that situation could be used to answer the problem today. However, there is no such past instance in this case. There are three disadvantages of looking up the data table:

1. As mentioned earlier, how to decide if there is not a row that corresponds to the exact situation today? If there is no matching instance available in the database, the past experience cannot guide the decision.

2. Searching through the entire past database may be time consuming, depending on the number of variables and the organization of the database.

3. What if the data values are not available for all the variables? In this instance, if the data for humidity variable was not available, looking up the past data would not help.

4. A better way of solving the problem may be to abstract the knowledge from the past data into decision tree or rules. These rules can be represented in a decision tree, and then that tree can be used to make the decisions. The decision tree may not need values for all the variables.

Decision Tree Construction

A tree is a hierarchically branched structure. What should be the first question asked in the tree? One should ask the most important question first, and the least important questions later. What is the most important question that should be asked to solve the problem? How is the importance of the questions determined? How should the root node of the tree be determined?

Determining root node of the tree: In this example, there are four choices of questions based on the four variables: what is the outlook, what is the temperature, what is the humidity, and what is the wind speed? A criterion should be used by which one of these questions gives the most insight about the situation. The criterion of frugality is a good one, that is, which question will provide us the shortest ultimate tree? Another way to look at this is that if one is allowed to ask only one question, which one would one ask? The most important question should be the one that, by itself, helps make the most correct decisions with the fewest errors. The four questions can be systematically compared, to see which variable helps make the most correct decisions. One should systematically calculate the correctness of decisions based on each question. Then, one can select the question with the fewest errors.

Start with any variable, in this case outlook. It can take three values: sunny, overcast, and rainy.

Start with the sunny value of outlook. There are five instances where the outlook is sunny. In two of the five instances, the *play* decision was *yes*, and in the other three, the decision was *no*. Thus, if the decision rule was that outlook: sunny → no, then three out of five decisions would be correct, while two out of five such decisions would be incorrect. There are two errors out of five. This can be recorded in Row 1.

Attribute	Rules	Error	Total Error
Outlook	Sunny → No	2/5	

Similar analysis would be done for other values of the outlook variable.

There are four instances where the outlook is overcast. In all four out of four instances, the *play* decision was *yes*. Thus, if the decision rule was that outlook: overcast → yes, then four out of four decisions would be correct, while none of the decisions would be incorrect. There are zero errors out of four. This can be recorded in the next row.

Attribute	Rules	Error	Total Error
Outlook	Sunny → No	2/5	
	Overcast → Yes	0/4	

There are five instances where the outlook is rainy. In three out of five instances, the *play* decision was *yes*, and in the other three, the decision was *no*. Thus, if the decision rule was that outlook: rainy ☒ yes, then three out of five decisions would be correct, while two out of five decisions would be incorrect. There will be two errors out of five. This can be recorded in next row.

Attribute	Rules	Error	Total Error
Outlook	Sunny → No	2/5	4/14
	Overcast → Yes	0/4	
	Rainy → Yes	2/5	

Adding up errors for all values of outlook, there are 4 errors out of 14.

A similar analysis can be done for the other three variables. At the end of that analytical exercise, the following error table will be constructed.

Attribute	Rules	Error	Total Error
Outlook	Sunny → No	2/5	4/14
	Overcast → Yes	0/4	
	Rainy → Yes	2/5	
Temp	Hot → No	2/4	5/14
	Mild → Yes	2/6	
	Cool → Yes	1/4	
Humidity	High → No	3/7	4/14
	Normal → Yes	1/7	
Windy	False → Yes	2/8	5/14
	True → No	3/6	

The variable that leads to the least number of errors (and thus the most number of correct decisions) should be chosen as the first node. In this case, two variables have the least number of errors. There is a tie between outlook and humidity, as both have 4 errors out of 14 instances. The tie can be broken using another criterion, the purity of resulting subtrees.

If all the errors were concentrated in a few of the subtrees, and some of the branches were completely free of error, which is preferred from a usability perspective. Outlook has one error-free branch, for the overcast value of outlook. There is no such pure subclass for humidity variable. Thus, the tie is broken in favor of outlook. The decision tree will use outlook as the first node or the first splitting variable. The first question that should be asked to solve the *play* problem is "What is the value of outlook?"

Splitting the tree: From the outlook node, the tree will split into three branches, or subtrees, corresponding to each of the three values of outlook. Data for the root node (the entire data) will be divided into the three segments, one for each of the value of outlook.

The sunny branch will inherit the data for the instances that had sunny as the value of outlook. These will be used for further building of that subtree. Similarly, the rainy branch will inherit data for the instances that had rainy as the value of outlook. These will be used for further building of that subtree. The overcast branch will inherit the data for the instances that had overcast as the outlook. However, there will be no need to build further on that branch. There is a clear decision, *yes*, for all instances when outlook value is overcast.

The decision tree will look like this after the first level of splitting. Thus, if one was allowed to ask only one question, this tree will help make the best decision.

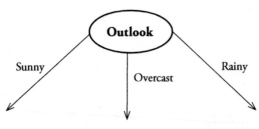

Temp	Humidity	Windy	Play
Hot	High	False	No
Hot	High	True	No
Mild	High	False	No
Cool	Normal	False	Yes
Mild	Normal	True	Yes

YES

Temp	Humidity	Windy	Play
Mild	High	False	Yes
Cool	Normal	False	Yes
Cool	Normal	True	No
Mild	Normal	False	Yes
Mild	High	True	No

Determining the next nodes of the tree: A similar logic of tree building should be applied to each branch. For the sunny branch on the left, error values will be calculated for the three other variables: temp, humidity, and windy. Final comparison looks like this:

Attribute	Rules	Error	Total Error
Temp	Hot → No	0/2	1/5
	Mild → No	1/2	
	Cool → Yes	0/1	
Humidity	High → No	0/3	0/5
	Normal → Yes	0/2	
Windy	False → No	1/3	2/5
	True → Yes	1/2	

The variable of humidity shows the least amount of error, that is, zero error. The other two variables have nonzero errors. Thus, the branch on the left will use humidity as the next split variable.

Similar analysis should be done for the "rainy" value of the tree. The final comparison would look as follows.

Attribute	Rules	Error	Total Error
Temp	Mild → Yes	1/3	2/5
	Cool → yes	1/2	
Humidity	High → No	1/2	1/5
	Normal → Yes	1/3	
Windy	False → Yes	0/3	0/5
	True → No	1/2	

For the *rainy* branch, it can similarly be seen that the variable *windy* gives all the correct answers, while none of the other two variables makes all the correct decisions.

This is how the final decision tree looks like. Here it is produced using Weka open-source data mining platform (Figure 5.1). This is the model that abstracts the knowledge of the past data of decision.

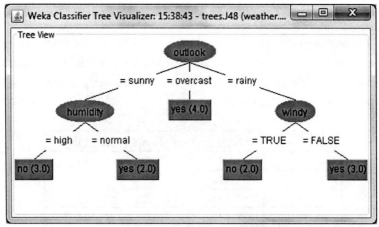

Figure 5.1 Decision tree for the weather problem

This tree can be used to solve the current problem. Here is the problem again.

Outlook	Temp	Humidity	Windy	Play
Sunny	Hot	Normal	True	?

According to the tree, the first question to ask is about outlook. In this problem, the outlook is sunny. So, the decision problem moves to the *sunny* branch of the tree. The node in that subtree is humidity. In the problem, humidity is normal. That branch leads to an answer *yes*. Thus, the answer to the *play* problem is *yes*.

Outlook	Temp	Humidity	Windy	Play
Sunny	Hot	Normal	True	Yes

Lessons from Constructing Trees

Here are some benefits of using this decision tree compared with looking up the answers from the data table (Table 5.1).

Table 5.1 Comparing decision tree with table lookup

	Decision Tree	Table Lookup
Accuracy	Varied level of accuracy	100% accurate
Generality	General; applies to all situations	Applies only when a similar case occurred before
Frugality	Only three variables needed	All four variables are needed
Simple	Only one or two questions asked	All four variable values are needed
Easy	Logical and easy to understand	Can be cumbersome to look up; no understanding of the logic behind the decision

Here are a few observations about how the tree was constructed:

1. This final decision tree has zero errors in mapping to the prior data. In other words, the tree completely fits the data; it has a predictive accuracy of 100 percent. In real-life situations, such perfect predictive accuracy is not possible when making decision trees. When there are larger, complicated data sets, with many more variables, a perfect fit is unachievable. This is especially true in business and social contexts, where things are not always fully clear and consistent.

2. The decision tree algorithm selected the minimum number of variables that are needed to solve the problem. Thus, one can start with

all available variables, and let the decision tree algorithm select what is useful, and discard the rest.

3. This tree is symmetric with all branches being of almost similar lengths. However, in real-life situations, some of the branches may be longer than the others.

4. It is possible to increase predictive accuracy by making more subtrees and making the tree longer. However, the marginal accuracy gained from each subsequent level in the tree will be less and may not be worth the loss in ease and interpretability of the tree. If the branches are long and complicated, it will be difficult to understand and use. The longer branches may need to be trimmed to keep the tree easy to use.

5. A perfectly fitting tree has the danger of overfitting the data, thus capturing all the random variations in the data. It may fit the training data well, but may not do well in predicting the future instances.

6. There was a single best tree for this data. There could however be two or more equally efficient decision trees of similar length with similar predictive accuracy for the same data set.

7. Decision trees are based strictly on observing patterns within the data, and do not rely on any underlying theory of the problem domain. When multiple candidate trees are available, they can all be used, wherever each one is more reflective for different situations. The ease of understanding the tree would be a criterion for selecting one tree. If both are equally intuitive, then use either one based on personal preference.

Decision Tree Algorithms

Decision trees employ the divide-and-conquer method. The data is branched at each node according to certain criteria until all the data is assigned to leaf nodes. It recursively divides a training set until each division consists of examples from one class.

The following is the pseudocode for making decision trees:

1. *Create a root node and assign all of the training data to it.*
2. *Select the best splitting attribute according to certain criteria.*
3. *Add a branch to the root node for each value of the split.*

> 4. *Split the data into mutually exclusive subsets along the lines of the specific split.*
> 5. *Repeat Steps 2 and 3 for each and every leaf node until the stopping criteria is reached.*

There are many algorithms for making decision trees. The most popular ones are C5, CART, and CHAID. They differ on three key elements:

1. *Splitting criteria*
   a. Which variable to use for the first split? How should one determine the most important variable for the first branch, and subsequently, for each subtree? There are many measures like least errors, information gain, and Gini coefficient.
   b. What values to use for the split? If the variables have continuous values, such as for age or BP, what value-ranges should be used to make bins?
   c. How many branches should be allowed for each node? There could be binary trees, with just two branches at each node. Or there could be more branches allowed.
2. *Stopping criteria*
   a. When to stop building the tree? There are two major ways to make that determination. The tree building could be stopped when a certain depth of the branches has been reached and the tree becomes unreadable after that. The tree could also be stopped when the error level at any node is within predefined tolerable levels.
3. *Pruning*
   a. Prepruning and postpruning: The tree could be trimmed to make it more balanced and more easily usable. The pruning is often done after the tree is constructed, to balance out the tree and improve usability.

In order to increase predictive accuracy, a decision tree may completely fit the training data and make the tree long. It will thus show good accuracy on training data. However, it may not show such good accuracy on test data. The symptoms of an overfitted tree are a tree too deep, with too many branches, some of which may reflect anomalies due to noise or outliers. Thus, the tree should be pruned. There are two approaches to avoid overfitting.

- Prepruning means to halt the tree construction early, when certain criteria are met. The downside is that it is difficult to decide what criteria to use for halting the construction, because we do not know what may happen subsequently, if we keep growing the tree.

- Postpruning: Remove branches or subtrees from a "fully grown" tree. This method is commonly used. C4.5 algorithm uses a statistical method to estimate the errors at each node for pruning. A validation set may be used for pruning as well (Table 5.2).

Table 5.2 Comparing popular decision tree algorithms

Decision Tree	C4.5	CART	CHAID
Full name	Iterative Dichotomiser (ID3)	Classification and regression trees	Chi-square automatic interaction detector
Basic algorithm	Hunt's algorithm	Hunt's algorithm	Adjusted significance testing
Developer	Ross Quinlan	Bremman	Gordon Kass
When developed	1986	1984	1980
Types of trees	Classification	Classification and regression trees	Classification and regression
Serial implementation	Tree growth and tree pruning	Tree growth and tree pruning	Tree growth and tree pruning
Type of data	Discrete and continuous; incomplete data	Discrete and continuous	Non-normal data also accepted
Types of splits	Multiway splits	Binary splits only; clever surrogate splits to reduce tree depth	Multiway splits as default
Splitting criteria	Information gain	Gini coefficient, and others	Chi-square test
Pruning criteria	Clever bottom-up technique avoids overfitting	Remove weakest links first	Trees can become very large
Implementation	Publicly available	Publicly available in most packages	Popular in market research, for segmentation

Conclusion

Decision trees are the most popular, versatile, and easy-to-use data mining technique with high predictive accuracy. They are also very useful as communication tools with executives. There are many successful decision tree algorithms. All publicly available data mining software platforms offer multiple decision tree implementations.

Review Questions

1. What is a decision tree? Why are decision trees the most popular classification technique?

2. What is a splitting variable? Describe three criteria for choosing splitting variable.

3. What is pruning? What are prepruning and postpruning? Why choose one over the other?

4. What are Gini coefficient and information gain? (Hint: google it.)

Hands-on exercise: Create a decision tree for the following data set. The objective is to predict the class category (loan approved or not).

Age	Job	House	Credit	Loan Approved
Young	False	No	Fair	No
Young	False	No	Good	No
Young	True	No	Good	Yes
Young	True	Yes	Fair	Yes
Young	False	No	Fair	No
Middle	False	No	Fair	No
Middle	False	No	Good	No
Middle	True	Yes	Good	Yes
Middle	False	Yes	Excellent	Yes
Middle	False	Yes	Excellent	Yes
Old	False	Yes	Excellent	Yes
Old	False	Yes	Good	Yes
Old	True	No	Good	Yes
Old	True	No	Excellent	Yes
Old	False	No	Fair	No

Then solve the following problem using the model.

Age	Job	House	Credit	Loan Approved
Young	False	No	Good	?

Liberty Stores Case Exercise: Step 4

Liberty is constantly evaluating requests for opening new stores. They would like to formalize the process for handling many requests so that the best candidates are selected for detailed evaluation.

Develop a decision tree for evaluating new stores options. Here is the training data:

City Size	Avg Income	Local Investors	LOHAS Awareness	Decision
Big	High	Yes	High	Yes
Med	Med	No	Med	No
Small	Low	Yes	Low	No
Big	High	No	High	Yes
Small	Med	Yes	High	No
Med	High	Yes	Med	Yes
Med	Med	Yes	Med	No
Big	Med	No	Med	No
Med	High	Yes	Low	No
Small	High	No	High	Yes
Small	Med	No	High	No
Med	High	No	Med	No

Use the decision tree to answer the following question.

City Size	Avg Income	Local Investors	LOHAS Awareness	Decision
Med	Med	No	Med	?

CHAPTER 6

Regression

Regression is a well-known statistical technique to model the predictive relationship between several independent variables (DVs) and one dependent variable. The objective is to find the best-fitting curve for a dependent variable in a multidimensional space, with each independent variable being a dimension. The curve could be a straight line, or it could be a nonlinear curve. The quality of fit of the curve to the data can be measured by a coefficient of correlation (r), which is the square root of the amount of variance explained by the curve.

The key steps for regression are simple:

1. List all the variables available for making the model.
2. Establish a dependent variable of interest.
3. Examine visual (if possible) relationships between variables of interest.
4. Find a way to predict dependent variable using the other variables.

Caselet: Data-Driven Prediction Markets

Traditional pollsters still seem to be using methodologies that worked well a decade or two ago. Nate Silver is a new breed of data-based political forecasters who are seeped in big data and advanced analytics. In the 2012 elections, he predicted that Obama would win the election with 291 electoral votes, compared to 247 for Mitt Romney, giving the President a 62-percent lead and re-election. He stunned the political forecasting world by correctly predicting the presidential winner in all 50 states, including all 9 swing states. He also correctly predicted the winner in 31 of the 33 U.S. Senate races.

Nate Silver brings a different view to the world of forecasting political elections, viewing it as a scientific discipline. State the hypothesis scientifically, gather all available information, analyze the data and extract insights using sophisticated models and algorithms, and finally, apply human judgment to interpret those insights. The results are likely to be much more grounded and successful. (Source: The Signal and the Noise: Why Most Predictions Fail but Some Don't, by Nate Silver, 2012)

Q1. *What is the impact of this story on traditional pollsters and commentators?*

Correlations and Relationships

Statistical relationships are about which elements of data hang together, and which ones hang separately. It is about categorizing variables that have a relationship with one another, and categorizing variables that are distinct and unrelated to other variables. It is about describing significant positive relationships and significant negative differences.

The first and foremost measure of the strength of a relationship is co-relation (or correlation). The strength of a correlation is a quantitative measure that is measured in a normalized range between 0 (zero) and 1. A correlation of 1 indicates a perfect relationship, where the two variables are in perfect sync. A correlation of 0 indicates that there is no relationship between the variables.

The relationship can be positive, or it can be an inverse relationship, that is, the variables may move together in the same direction or in the opposite direction. Therefore, a good measure of correlation is the correlation coefficient, which is the square root of correlation. This coefficient, called r, can thus range from -1 to $+1$. An r value of 0 signifies no relationship. An r value of 1 shows perfect relationship in the same direction, and an r value of -1 shows a perfect relationship but moving in opposite directions.

Given two numeric variables x and y, the coefficient of correlation r is mathematically computed by the following equation. $\bar{x}$ is the mean of x, and $\bar{y}$ is the mean of y.

$$r = \frac{[(x - \bar{x})][(y - \bar{y})]}{\sqrt{[(x - \bar{x})^2][(y - \bar{y})^2]}}$$

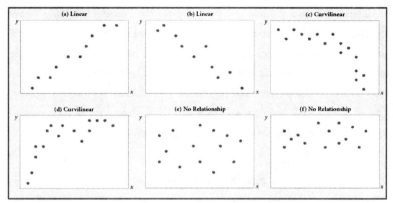

Figure 6.1 Scatter plots showing types of relationships among two variables

(*Source*: Groebner et al. 2013)

Visual Look at Relationships

A scatter plot (or scatter diagram) is a simple exercise for plotting all data points between two variables on a two-dimensional graph. It provides a visual layout of where all the data points are placed in that two-dimensional space. The scatter plot can be useful for graphically intuiting the relationship between two variables.

Here is a picture that shows many possible patterns in scatter diagrams (Figure 6.1).

Chart (a) shows a very strong linear relationship between the variables x and y. That means the value of y increases proportionally with x. Chart (b) also shows a strong linear relationship between the variables x and y. Here it is an inverse relationship. That means the value of y decreases proportionally with x.

Chart (c) shows a curvilinear relationship. It is an inverse relationship, which means that the value of y decreases proportionally with x. However, it seems a relatively well-defined relationship, like an arc of a circle, which can be represented by a simple quadratic equation (quadratic means the power of two, that is, using terms like x^2 and y^2). Chart (d) shows a positive curvilinear relationship. However, it does not seem to resemble a regular shape, and thus would not be a strong relationship. Charts (e) and (f) show no relationship. That means variables x and y are independent of each other.

Charts (a) and (b) are good candidates that model a simple linear regression model (the terms regression model and regression equation can be used interchangeably). Chart (c) too could be modeled with a little more complex, quadratic regression equation. Chart (d) might require an even higher order polynomial regression equation to represent the data. Charts (e) and (f) have no relationship, thus, they cannot be modeled together, by regression or using any other modeling tool.

Regression Exercise

The regression model is described as a linear equation that follows. y is the dependent variable, that is, the variable being predicted. x is the independent variable, or the predictor variable. There could be many predictor variables (such as $x1, x2, \ldots$) in a regression equation. However, there can be only one dependent variable (y) in the regression equation.

$$y = \beta_0 + \beta_1 x + \varepsilon$$

A simple example of a regression equation would be to predict a house price from the size of the house. Here are sample house data:

House Price	Size (sqft)
$229,500	1,850
$273,300	2,190
$247,000	2,100
$195,100	1,930
$261,000	2,300
$179,700	1,710
$168,500	1,550
$234,400	1,920
$168,800	1,840
$180,400	1,720
$156,200	1,660
$288,350	2,405
$186,750	1,525
$202,100	2,030
$256,800	2,240

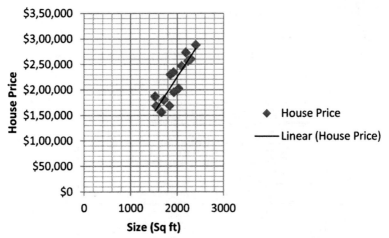

Figure 6.2 Scatter plot and regression equation between House price and house size

The two dimensions of (one predictor, one outcome variable) data can be plotted on a scatter diagram. A scatter plot with a best-fitting line looks like the graph that follows (Figure 6.2).

Visually, one can see a positive correlation between house price and size (sqft). However, the relationship is not perfect. Running a regression model between the two variables produces the following output (truncated).

Regression Statistics	
Multiple r	0.891
r^2	0.794
	Coefficients
Intercept	-54,191
Size (sqft)	139.48

It shows the coefficient of correlation is 0.891. r^2, the measure of total variance explained by the equation, is 0.794, or 79 percent. That means the two variables are moderately and positively correlated. Regression coefficients help create the following equation for predicting house prices.

House Price (\$) = 139.48 × Size (sqft) − 54,191

This equation explains only 79 percent of the variance in house prices. Suppose other predictor variables are made available, such as the number of rooms in the house, it might help improve the regression model.

The house data now looks like this:

House Price	Size (sqft)	# Rooms
$229,500	1,850	4
$273,300	2,190	5
$247,000	2,100	4
$195,100	1,930	3
$261,000	2,300	4
$179,700	1,710	2
$168,500	1,550	2
$234,400	1,920	4
$168,800	1,840	2
$180,400	1,720	2
$156,200	1,660	2
$288,350	2,405	5
$186,750	1,525	3
$202,100	2,030	2
$256,800	2,240	4

While it is possible to make a three-dimensional scatter plot, one can alternatively examine the correlation matrix among the variables.

	House Price	Size (sqft)	# Rooms
House Price	1		
Size (sqft)	0.891	1	
Rooms	0.944	0.748	1

It shows that the house price has a strong correlation with number of rooms (0.944) as well. Thus, it is likely that adding this variable to the regression model will add to the strength of the model.

Running a regression model between these three variables produces the following output.

Regression Statistics	
Multiple r	0.984
r^2	0.968
	Coefficients
Intercept	12,923
Size(sqft)	65.60
Rooms	23,613

It shows the coefficient of correlation of this regression model is 0.984. r^2, the total variance explained by the equation, is 0.968, or 97 percent. That means the variables are positively and very strongly correlated. Adding a new relevant variable has helped improve the strength of the regression model.

Using the regression coefficients helps create the following equation for predicting house prices.

House Price (\$) = 65.6 × Size (sqft) + 23,613 × Rooms + 12,924

This equation shows a 97-percent goodness-of-fit with the data, which is very good for business and economic data. There is always some random variation in naturally occurring business data, and it is not desirable to overfit the model to the data.

This predictive equation should be used for future transactions. Given a situation that follows, it will be possible to calculate the price of the house with 2,000 sqft and 3 rooms.

House Price	Size (sqft)	# Rooms
?	2,000	3

House Price (\$) = 65.6 × 2,000 (sqft) + 23,613 × 3 + 12,924 = \$214,963

The predicted values should be compared to the actual values to see how close the model is able to predict the actual value. As new data points become available, there are opportunities to fine-tune and improve the model.

Nonlinear Regression Exercise

The relationship between the variables may also be curvilinear. For example, given past data from electricity consumption (kWh) and temperature (temp), the objective is to predict the electrical consumption from the temperature value. Here are a dozen past observations.

KWatts	Temp (F)
12,530	46.8
10,800	52.1
10,180	55.1
9,730	59.2
9,750	61.9
10,230	66.2
11,160	69.9
13,910	76.8
15,690	79.3
15,110	79.7
17,020	80.2
17,880	83.3

In two dimensions (one predictor, one outcome variable), data can be plotted on a scatter diagram. A scatter plot with a best-fitting line looks like the graph that follows (Figure 6.3).

It is visually clear that the first line does not fit the data well. The relationship between temperature and Kwatts follows a curvilinear model,

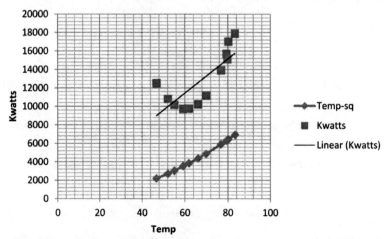

Figure 6.3 Scatter plots showing regression between (a) Kwatts and temp, and (b) Kwatts and temp-sq

where it hits bottom at a certain value of temperature. The regression model confirms the relationship since r is only 0.77 and r^2 is also only 60 percent. Thus, only 60 percent of the variance is explained.

The regression model can then be enhanced using a temp-sq variable in the equation. The second line is the relationship between kWh and temp-sq. Visually plotting the energy consumption shows a strong linear relationship with the quadratic temp-sq variable.

Running the regression model after adding the quadratic variable leads to the following results:

Regression Statistics	
Multiple r	0.992
r^2	0.984
	Coefficients
Intercept	67,245
Temp (F)	−1,911
Temp-sq	15.87

It shows that the coefficient of correlation of the regression model is now 0.99. r^2, the total variance explained by the equation, is 0.985, or 98.5 percent. That means the variables are very strongly and positively correlated. The regression coefficients help create the following equation for

Energy Consumption = 15.87 × temp-sq − 1,911 × Temp + 67,245

This equation shows a 98.5-percent fit, which is very good for business and economic contexts. Now one can predict the Kwatts value for when the temperature is 72 degrees.

Energy consumption = (15.87 × 72 × 72) − (1,911 × 72) + 67,245 = 11,923 Kwatts

Logistic Regression

Regression models traditionally work with continuous numeric value data for dependent and independent variables. Logistic regression models can, however, work with dependent variables with binary values, such as whether a loan is approved (yes or no). Logistic regression measures the relationship between a categorical dependent variable and one or more independent variables. For example, logistic regression might be used to predict whether a patient has a given disease (e.g., diabetes), based on observed characteristics of the patient (age, gender, body mass index, results of blood tests, etc.).

Logistical regression models use probability scores as the predicted values of the dependent variable. Logistic regression takes the natural logarithm of the odds of the dependent variable being a case (referred to as the logit) to create a continuous criterion as a transformed version of the dependent variable. Thus, the logit transformation is used in logistic regression as the dependent variable. The net effect is that although the dependent variable in logistic regression is binomial (or categorical, i.e., has only two possible values), the logit is the continuous function upon which linear regression is conducted. Here is the general logistic function, with independent variable on the horizontal axis and the logit dependent variable on the vertical axis (Figure 6.4).

All popular data mining platforms provide support for regular multiple regression models, as well as options for logistic regression.

Advantages and Disadvantages of Regression Models

Regression models are very popular because they offer many advantages.

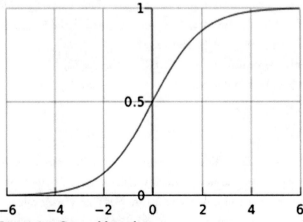

Figure 6.4 General logit function

1. Regression models are easy to understand as they are built upon basic statistical principles, such as correlation and least square error.

2. Regression models provide simple algebraic equations that are easy to understand and use.

3. The strength (or the goodness of fit) of the regression model is measured in terms of the correlation coefficients, and other related statistical parameters that are well understood.

4. Regression models can match and beat the predictive power of other modeling techniques.

5. Regression models can include all the variables that one wants to include in the model.

6. Regression modeling tools are pervasive. They are found in statistical packages as well as data mining packages. MS Excel spreadsheets can also provide simple regression modeling capabilities.

Regression models can however prove inadequate under many circumstances.

1. Regression models cannot cover for poor data quality issues. If the data is not prepared well to remove missing values, or is not well-behaved in terms of a normal distribution, the validity of the model suffers.

2. Regression models suffer from collinear problems (meaning strong linear correlations among some independent variables). If the independent variables have strong correlations among themselves, then they will eat into each other's predictive power and the regression coefficients will lose their ruggedness.

3. Regression models will not automatically choose between highly collinear variables, although some packages attempt to do that. Regression models can be unwieldy and unreliable if a large number of variables are included in the model. All variables entered into the model will be reflected in the regression equation, irrespective of their contribution to the predictive power of the model. There is no concept of automatic pruning the model.

4. Regression models do not automatically take care of nonlinearity. The user needs to imagine the kind of additional terms that might be needed to be added to the regression model to improve its fit.

5. Regression models work only with numeric data and not with categorical variables. There are ways to deal with categorical variables though by creating multiple new variables with a yes/no value.

Conclusion

Regression models are simple, versatile, visual/graphical tools with high predictive ability. They include nonlinear as well as binary predictions. Regression models should be used in conjunction with other data mining techniques to confirm the findings.

Review Exercises

1. What is a regression model?
2. What is a scatter plot? How does it help?
3. Compare and contrast decision trees with regression models?
4. Using the data that follows, create a regression model to predict the Test 2 from the Test 1 score. Then predict the score for one who got a 46 in Test 1.

Test 1	Test 2
59	56
52	63
44	55
51	50
42	66
42	48
41	58
45	36
27	13
63	50
54	81
44	56
50	64
47	50

Liberty Stores Case Exercise: Step 5

Liberty wants to forecast its sales for next year for financial budgeting.

Year	Global GDP Index per Capita	# Cust Serv Calls ('000s)	# Employees ('000)	# Items ('000)	Revenue ($M)
1	100	25	45	11	2,000
2	112	27	53	11	2,400
3	115	22	54	12	2,700
4	123	27	58	14	2,900
5	122	32	60	14	3,200
6	132	33	65	15	3,500
7	143	40	72	16	4,000
8	126	30	65	16	4,200
9	166	34	85	17	4,500
10	157	47	97	18	4,700
11	176	33	98	18	4,900
12	180	45	100	20	5,000

1. Compute the correlations. Which variables are strongly correlated?
2. Create a regression model that best predicts the revenue.

CHAPTER 7

Artificial Neural Networks

Artificial neural networks (ANNs) are inspired by the information processing model of the mind/brain. The human brain consists of billions of neurons that link with one another in an intricate pattern. Every neuron receives information from many other neurons, processes it, gets excited or not, and passes its state information to other neurons.

Just like the brain is a multipurpose system, so also the ANNs are very versatile systems. They can be used for many kinds of pattern recognition and prediction. They are also used for classification, regression, clustering, association, and optimization activities. They are used in finance, marketing, manufacturing, operations, information systems applications, and so on.

ANNs are composed of a large number of highly interconnected processing elements (neurons) working in a multilayered structures that receive inputs, process the inputs, and produce an output. An ANN is designed for a specific application, such as pattern recognition or data classification, and trained through a learning process. Just like in biological systems, ANNs make adjustments to the synaptic connections with each learning instance.

ANNs are like a black box trained into solving a particular type of problem, and they can develop high predictive powers. Their intermediate synaptic parameter values evolve as the system obtains feedback on its predictions, and thus an ANN learns from more training data (Figure 7.1).

Figure 7.1 General ANN model

Caselet: IBM Watson—Analytics in Medicine

The amount of medical information available is doubling every five years and much of this data is unstructured. Physicians simply do not have time to read every journal that can help them keep up-to-date with the latest advances. Mistakes in diagnosis are likely to happen, and clients have become more aware of the evidence. Analytics will transform the field of medicine into evidence-based medicine. How can health care providers address these problems?

IBM's Watson cognitive computing system can analyze large amounts of unstructured text and develop hypotheses based on that analysis. Physicians can use Watson to assist in diagnosing and treating patients. First, the physician might describe symptoms and other related factors to the system. Watson can then identify the key pieces of information and mine the patient's data to find relevant facts about family history, current medications, and other existing conditions. It combines this information with current findings from tests, and then forms and tests a hypotheses by examining a variety of data sources—treatment guidelines, electronic medical record (EMR) data, and doctors' and nurses' notes, as well as peer-reviewed research and clinical studies. From here, Watson can provide potential treatment options and its confidence rating for each suggestion.

Watson has been deployed at many leading health care institutions to improve the quality and efficiency of health care decisions; to help clinicians uncover insights from its patient information in electronic medical records; among other benefits.

Q1. How would IBM Watson change medical practices in the future?

Q2. In what other industries and functions could this technology be applied?

Business Applications of ANN

Neural networks are used most often when the objective function is complex and where there exists plenty of data, and the model is expected to improve over a period of time.

1. They are used in stock price prediction where the rules of the game are extremely complicated, and a lot of data needs to be processed very quickly.
2. They are used for character recognition, as in recognizing handwritten text, or damaged or mangled text. They are used in recognizing finger prints. These are complicated patterns and are unique for each person. Layers of neurons can progressively clarify the pattern.
3. They are also used in traditional classification problems, such as approving a loan application.

Design Principles of an ANN

1. A neuron is the basic processing unit of the network. The neuron (or processing element) receives inputs from its preceding neurons (or PEs), does some nonlinear weighted computation on the basis of those inputs, transforms the result into its output value, and then passes on the output to the next neuron in the network (Figure 7.2). X's are the inputs, w's are the weights for each input, and y is the output.

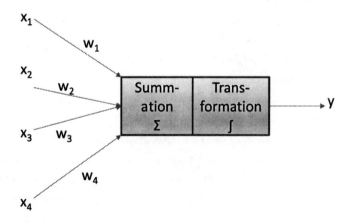

Figure 7.2 Block diagram Model for a single artificial neuron

2. A neural network is a multilayered model. There is at least one input neuron, one output neuron, and at least one processing neuron. An

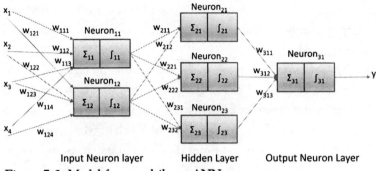

Figure 7.3 Model for a multilayer ANN

ANN with just this basic structure would be a simple, single-stage computational unit. A simple task may be processed by just that one neuron and the result may be communicated soon. ANNs, however, may have multiple layers of processing elements in sequence. There could be many neurons involved in a sequence depending upon the complexity of the predictive action. The layers of PEs could work in sequence, or they could work in parallel (Figure 7.3).

3. The processing logic of each neuron may assign different weights to the various incoming input streams. The processing logic may also use nonlinear transformation, such as a sigmoid function, from the processed values to the output value. This processing logic and the intermediate weight and processing functions are just what works for the system as a whole, in its objective of solving a problem collectively. Thus, the neural networks are considered to be an opaque and a black-box system.

4. The neural network can be trained by making similar decisions over and over again with many training cases. It will continue to learn by adjusting its internal computation and communication based on feedback about its previous decisions. Thus, the neural networks become better at making a decision as they handle more and more decisions.

Depending upon the nature of the problem and the availability of good training data, at some point the neural network will learn enough and begin to match the predictive accuracy of a human expert. In many practical situations, the predictions of ANN, trained over a long period of time with a large number of training data, have begun to decisively become more accurate than human experts. At that point, ANN can begin to be seriously considered for deployment in real situations in real time.

Representation of a Neural Network

A neural network is a series of neurons (or processing elements) that receive inputs from other neurons. They do a weighted summation function of all the inputs, using different weights (or importance) for each input. The weighted sum is then transformed into an output value using a transfer function.

Learning in ANN occurs when the various processing elements in the neural network adjust the underlying relationship (weights, transfer function, etc.) between input and outputs, in response to the feedback on their predictions. If the prediction made was correct, then the weights would remain the same, but if the prediction was incorrect, then the parameter values would change.

The transformation (transfer) function is any function suitable for the task at hand. It can be a linear function, by converting the value to a smaller or larger value. The transfer function could be a nonlinear sigmoid function. Thus, if the normalized computed value is less than some value (say 0.5), then the output value will be zero. If the computed value is at the cut-off threshold, then the output value will be 1. It could be a nonlinear hyperbolic function in which the output is either -1 or 1. Many other functions could be designed for any or all of the processing elements.

Thus, in a neural network, every processing element can potentially have a different number of input values, a different set of weights for those inputs, and a different kind of transformation function. Those values support and compensate for one another until the neural network as a whole learns to provide the correct output, as desired by the user.

Architecting an Artificial Neural Network

There are many ways to architect the functioning of an ANN using fairly simple and open rules with a tremendous amount of flexibility at each stage. The most popular architecture is a feedforward, multilayered

ANN architectures for different applications	
Classification	Feedforward networks (MLP), radial basis function, and probabilistic
Regression	Feedforward networks (MLP), radial basis function
Clustering	Adaptive resonance theory (ART), Self-organizing maps (SOMs)
Association Rule Mining	Hopfield networks

perceptron (MLP) with back-propagation learning algorithm. That means there are multiple layers of PEs in the system, and the output of neurons is fed forward to the PEs in the next layers; and the feedback on the prediction is fed back into the neural network for learning to occur. This is essentially what was described in the earlier paragraphs.

Developing an ANN

It takes resources, training data, and skill and time to develop a neural network. Most data mining platforms offer at least the MLP algorithm to implement a neural network. The steps required to build an ANN are as follows:

1. Gather data: Divide into training data and test data. The training data needs to be further divided into training data and validation data.
2. Select the network architecture, such as feedforward network.
3. Select the algorithm, such as Multilayer Perception.
4. Set network parameters.
5. Train the ANN with training data.
6. Validate the model with validation data.
7. Freeze the weights and other parameters.
8. Test the trained network with test data.
9. Deploy the ANN when it achieves good predictive accuracy.

Other neural network architectures include probabilistic networks and self-organizing feature maps.

Training an ANN: Training data is split into three parts	
Training set	This data set is used to adjust the weights on the neural network (~ 60%).
Validation set	This data set is used to minimize overfitting and verifying accuracy (~ 20%).
Testing set	This data set is used only for testing the final solution in order to confirm the actual predictive power of the network (~ 20%).
k-fold cross-validation	approach means that the data is divided into k equal pieces, and the learning process is repeated k-times with each pieces becoming the training set. This process leads to less bias and more accuracy, but is more time consuming.

Here is the pseudocode for the Self-organizing Maps Algorithm

1. *Initialize each node's weights.*
2. *Present a randomly selected input vector to the lattice.*
3. *Determine most resembling (winning) node.*
4. *Determine the neighboring nodes.*
5. *Adjust the winning and neighboring nodes (make them more like the input vector)*
6. *Repeat steps 2-5 for until a stopping criteria is reached*

Advantages and Disadvantages of Using ANNs

There are many advantages of using ANN.

1. ANNs impose very little restrictions on their use. ANN can deal with (identify/model) highly nonlinear relationships on their own, without much work from the user or analyst. They help find practical data-driven solutions where algorithmic solutions are nonexistent or too complicated.
2. There is no need to program ANN neural networks, as they learn from examples. They get better with use, without much programing effort.

3. ANN can handle a variety of problem types, including classification, clustering, associations, and so on.
4. ANNs are tolerant of data quality issues, and they do not restrict the data to follow strict normality and/or independence assumptions.
5. ANN can handle both numerical and categorical variables.
6. ANNs can be much faster than other techniques.
7. Most importantly, ANN usually provide better results (prediction and/or clustering) compared to statistical counterparts, once they have been trained enough.

The key disadvantages arise from the fact that they are not easy to interpret or explain or compute.

1. They are deemed to be black-box solutions, lacking explainability.
2. Optimal design of ANN is still an art: It requires expertise and extensive experimentation.
3. It can be difficult to handle a large number of variables (especially the rich nominal attributes) with an ANN.
4. It takes large data sets to train an ANN.

Conclusion

ANNs are complex systems that mirror the functioning of the human brain. They are versatile enough to solve many data mining tasks with high accuracy. However, they are like black boxes and they provide little guidance on the intuitive logic behind their predictions.

Review Exercises

1. What is a neural network? How does it work?
2. Compare a neural network with a decision tree.
3. What makes a neural network versatile enough for supervised as well as unsupervised learning tasks?
4. Examine the steps in developing a neural network for predicting stock prices. What kind of objective function and what kind of data would be required for a good stock price predictor system using ANN?

CHAPTER 8

Cluster Analysis

Cluster analysis is used for automatic identification of natural groupings of things. It is also known as the segmentation technique. In this technique, data instances that are similar to (or near) each other are categorized into one cluster. Similarly, data instances that are very different (or far away) from each other are moved into different clusters.

Clustering is an unsupervised learning technique as there is no output or dependent variable for which a right or wrong answer can be computed. The correct number of clusters or the definition of those clusters is not known ahead of time. Clustering techniques can only suggest to the user how many clusters would make sense from the characteristics of the data. The user can specify a different, larger or smaller, number of desired clusters based on their making business sense. The cluster analysis technique will then define many distinct clusters from analysis of the data, with cluster definitions for each of those clusters. However, there are good cluster definitions, depending on how closely the cluster parameters fit the data.

Caselet: Cluster Analysis

A national insurance company distributes its personal and small commercial insurance products through independent agents. They wanted to increase their sales by better understanding their customers. They were interested in increasing their market share by doing some direct marketing campaigns, however without creating a channel conflict with the independent agents. They were also interested in examining different customer segments based on their needs, and the profitability of each of those segments.

They gathered attitudinal, behavioral, and demographic data using a mail survey of 2000 U.S. households that own auto insurance. Additional geodemographic and credit information was added to the survey data. Cluster analysis of the data revealed five roughly equal segments:

- *Non-Traditionals: interested in using the Internet and/or buying insurance at work.*
- *Direct Buyers: interested in buying via direct mail or telephone.*
- *Budget Conscious: interested in minimal coverage and finding the best deal.*
- *Agent Loyals: expressed strong loyalty to their agents and high levels of personal service.*
- *Hassle-Free: similar to Agent Loyals but less interested in face-to-face service.*

Q1. *Which customer segments would you choose for direct marketing? Will these create a channel conflict?*

Q2. *Could this segmentation apply to other service businesses? Which ones?*

(Source: greenbook.org)

Applications of Cluster Analysis

Cluster analysis is used in almost every field where there is a large variety of transactions. It helps provide characterization, definition, and labels for populations. It can help identify natural groupings of customers, products, patients, and so on. It can also help identify outliers in a specific domain and thus decrease the size and complexity of problems. A prominent business application of cluster analysis is in market research. Customers are segmented into clusters based on their characteristics—wants and needs, geography, price sensitivity, and so on.

Here are some examples of clustering:

1. *Market segmentation:* Categorizing customers according to their similarities, for example by their common wants and needs and propensity to pay, can help with targeted marketing.
2. *Product portfolio:* People of similar sizes can be grouped together to make small, medium, and large sizes for clothing items.

3. *Text mining:* Clustering can help organize a given collection of text documents according to their content similarities into clusters of related topics.

Definition of a Cluster

An operational definition of a cluster is that, given a representation of n objects, find K groups based on a measure of similarity, such that objects within the same group are alike but the objects in different groups are not alike.

However, the notion of similarity can be interpreted in many ways. Clusters are patterns, and there can be many kinds of patterns. Some clusters are traditional clusters, such as data points hanging together. However, there are other clusters, such as all points representing the circumference of a circle. There may be concentric circles with points of different circles representing different clusters. Clusters can differ in terms of their shape, size, and density. The presence of noise in the data makes the detection of the clusters even more difficult.

An ideal cluster can be defined as a set of points that is compact and isolated. In reality, a cluster is a subjective entity whose significance and interpretation requires domain knowledge. In the sample data what follows, how many clusters can one visualize? (refer Figure 8.1 below)

It seems like there are three clusters of approximately equal sizes. However, they can be seen as two clusters, depending on how we draw the dividing line. There is not a "truly optimal" way to calculate it. Heuristics are often used to define the number of clusters.

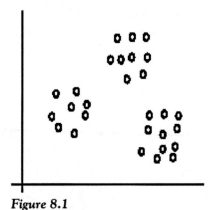

Figure 8.1

Representing Clusters

The clusters can be represented by a central or modal value. A cluster can be defined as the "centroid" of the collection of points belonging to it. A centroid is a measure of central tendency. It is the point from where the sum total of squared distance from all the points is the minimum. A real-life equivalent would be the city center as the point that is considered the most easy to use by all constituents of the city. Thus, all cities are defined by their centers or downtown areas.

A cluster can also be represented by the most frequently occurring value in the cluster, that is, the cluster can defined by its modal value. Thus, a particular cluster representing a social point of view could be called the "soccer mom's group," even though not all members of that cluster need currently be a mom with soccer-playing children.

Clustering Techniques

Cluster analysis is a machine-learning technique. The quality of a clustering result depends on the *algorithm*, the *distance* function, and the *application*. First, consider the distance function. Most cluster analysis methods use a distance measure to calculate the closeness between pairs of items. There are two major measures of distances: Euclidian distance ("as the crow flies" or straight line) is the most intuitive measure. The other popular measure is the Manhattan (rectilinear) distance, where one can go only in orthogonal directions. The Euclidian distance is the hypotenuse of a right triangle, while the Manhattan distance is the sum of the two legs of the right triangle.

In either case, the key objective of the clustering algorithm is the same:

- Interclusters distance ⇒ maximized
- Intraclusters distance ⇒ minimized

There are many algorithms to produce clusters. There are top-down, hierarchical methods that start with creating a given number of best-fitting clusters. There are also bottom-up methods that begin with identifying naturally occurring clusters.

The most popular clustering algorithm is the K-means algorithm. It is a top-down, statistical technique, based on the method of minimizing the least squared distance from the center points of the clusters. Machine-learning techniques, such as neural networks, are also used for clustering. Comparing cluster algorithms is a difficult task as there is no single right number of clusters!

Here is the generic pseudocode for clustering

1. *Pick an arbitrary number of groups/segments to be created.*
2. *Start with some initial randomly chosen center values for groups.*
3. *Classify instances to closest groups.*
4. *Compute new values for the group centers.*
5. *Repeat Steps 3 and 4 till groups converge.*
6. *If clusters are not satisfactory, go to Step 1 and pick a different number of groups/segments.*

The clustering exercise can be continued with a different number of clusters and different location of those points. Clusters are considered good if the cluster definitions stabilize, and the stabilized definitions prove useful for the purpose at hand. Else, repeat the clustering exercise with a different number of clusters and different starting points for group means.

Clustering Exercise

Here is a simple exercise to visually and intuitively identify clusters from data. X and Y are two dimensions of interest. The objective is to determine the number of clusters and the center points of those clusters.

X	Y
2	4
2	6
5	6
4	7
8	3
6	6
5	2
5	7
6	3
4	4

A scatter plot of 10 data points in 2 dimensions shows them distributed fairly randomly (Figure 8.2). As a bottom-up technique, the number of clusters and their centroids can be intuited.

The points are distributed randomly enough that it could be considered as one cluster. The circle would represent the central point (centroid) of these points.

However, there is a big distance between the points (2,6) and (8,3). So, this data could be broken into two clusters. The three points at the bottom right could form one cluster and the other seven could form the other cluster. The two clusters would look like this (Figure 8.3). The circles will be the new centroids.

The bigger cluster seems too far apart. So, it seems like the four points on the top will form a separate cluster. The three clusters could look like this (Figure 8.4).

This solution has three clusters. The cluster on the right is far from the other two clusters. However, its centroid is not too close to all the data points. The cluster at the top looks very tight-fitting, with a nice centroid. The third cluster, at the left, is spread out and may not be of much usefulness.

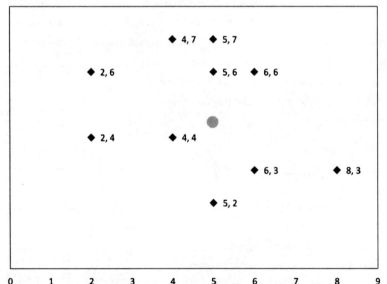

Figure 8.2 Initial data points and the centroid (shown as thick dot)

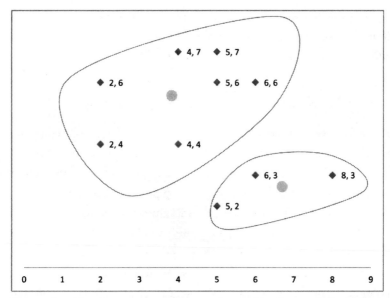

Figure 8.3 Dividing into two clusters (centroids shown as thick dots)

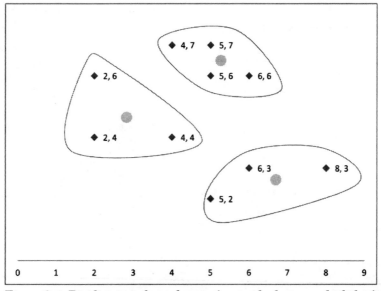

Figure 8.4 Dividing into three clusters (centroids shown as thick dots)

This was an exercise in producing three best-fitting cluster definitions from the given data. The right number of clusters will depend on the data and the application for which the data would be used.

K-Means Algorithm for Clustering

K-means is the most popular clustering algorithm. It iteratively computes the clusters and their centroids. It is a top-down approach to clustering. Starting with a given number of K clusters, say 3 clusters; thus, three random centroids will be created as starting points of the centers of three clusters (Figure 8.5). The circles are initial cluster centroids.

Step 1: For a data point, distance values will be from each of the three centroids. The data point will be assigned to the cluster with the shortest distance to the centroid. All data points will thus be assigned to one data point or the other. The arrows from each data element show the centroid that the point is assigned to (Figure 8.6).

Step 2: The centroid for each cluster will now be recalculated such that it is closest to all the data points allocated to that cluster. The dashed arrows show the centroids being moved from their old (shaded) values to the revised new values (Figure 8.7).

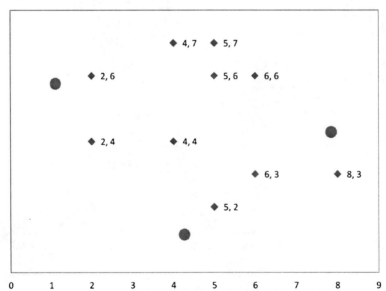

Figure 8.5 Randomly assigning three centroids for three data clusters

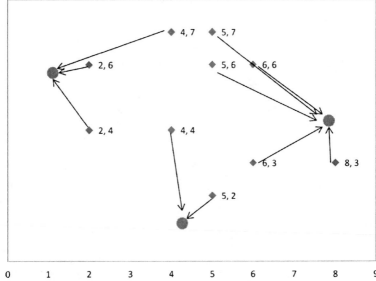

Figure 8.6 Assigning data points to closest centroid

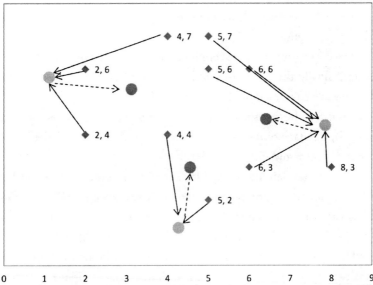

Figure 8.7 Recomputing centroids for each cluster

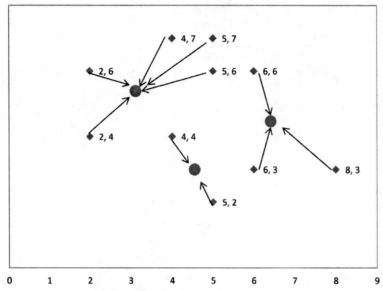

Figure 8.8 *Assigning data points to Recomputed centroids*

Step 3: Once again, data points are assigned to the three centroids closest to it (Figure 8.8).

The new centroids will be computed from the data points in the cluster until finally the centroids stabilize in their locations. These are the three clusters computed by this algorithm (Figure 8.9).

The three clusters shown are a 3-datapoints cluster with centroid (6.5,4.5), a 2-datapoint cluster with centroid (4.5,3), and a 5-datapoint cluster with centroid (3.5,3).

These cluster definitions are different from the ones derived visually. This is a function of the random starting centroid values. The centroid points used earlier in the visual exercise were different from that chosen with the K-means clustering algorithm. The K-means clustering exercise should, therefore, be run again with this data, but with new random centroid starting values. With many runs, the cluster definitions are likely to stabilize. If the cluster definitions do not stabilize, that may be a sign that the number of clusters chosen is too high or too low. The algorithm should also be run with different values of K.

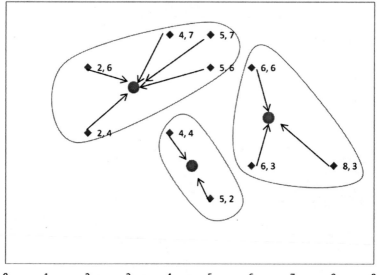

Figure 8.9 *Recomputing centroids for each cluster till clusters stabilize*

Here is the pseudocode for implementing a K-means algorithm.
   Algorithm K-Means (K number of clusters, D list of data points)

   1. *Choose K number of random data points as initial centroids (cluster centers).*
   2. *Repeat till cluster centers stabilize:*
      a. Allocate each point in D to the nearest of K centroids.
      b. Compute centroid for the cluster using all points in the cluster.

Selecting the Number of Clusters

The correct choice of the value of K is often ambiguous. It depends on the shape and scale of the distribution points in a data set and the desired clustering resolution of the user. Heuristics are needed to pick the right number. One can graph the percentage of variance explained by the clusters against the number of clusters. The first clusters will add more information (explain a lot of variance), but at some point the marginal gain in

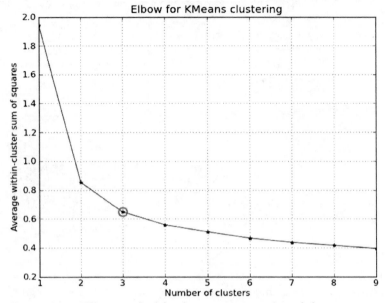

Figure 8.10 Elbow method for determining number of clusters in a data set

variance will fall, giving a sharp angle to the graph, looking like an elbow. At that elbow point, adding more clusters will not add much incremental value. That would be the desired value of K (Figure 8.10).

To engage with the data and to understand the clusters better, it is often better to start with a small number of clusters, such as 2 or 3, depending upon the data set and the application domain. The number can be increased subsequently, as needed from an application point of view. This helps understand the data and the clusters progressively better.

Advantages and Disadvantages of K-Means Algorithm

There are many advantages of **K-Means Algorithm**

1. K-means algorithm is simple, easy to understand, and easy to implement.
2. It is also efficient, in which the time taken to cluster K-means rises linearly with the number of data points.
3. No other clustering algorithm performs better than K-means, in general.

There are many disadvantages of **K-Means Algorithm**

1. The user needs to specify an initial value of K.
2. The process of finding the clusters may not converge.
3. It is not suitable for discovering clusters that are not hyperellipsoids (or hyperspheres).

Cluster analysis can also be done using ANN with the appropriative objective function. Neural networks can also be deployed for clustering, using the appropriate objective function. The neural network will produce the appropriate cluster centroids and cluster population for each cluster.

Conclusion

Cluster analysis is a useful, unsupervised learning technique that is used in many business situations to segment the data into meaningful small groups. K-means algorithm is an easy statistical technique to iteratively segment the data. However, there is only a heuristic technique to select the right number of clusters.

Review Exercises

1. What is unsupervised learning? When is it used?
2. Describe three business applications in your industry where cluster analysis will be useful.
3. Data about height and weight for a few volunteers is available. Create a set of clusters for the following data, to decide how many sizes of T-shirts should be ordered.

Height	Weight
71	165
68	165
72	180
67	113
72	178
62	101
70	150
69	172
72	185
63	149
69	132
61	115

Liberty Stores Case Exercise: Step 6

Liberty *wants* to find suitable number of segments for its customers, for targeted marketing. Here is a list of representative customers.

Cust #	# of transactions	Total Purchase ($)	Income ($ K)
1	5	450	90
2	10	800	82
3	15	900	77
4	2	50	30
5	18	900	60
6	9	200	45
7	14	500	82
8	8	300	22
9	7	250	90
10	9	1,000	80
11	1	30	60
12	6	700	80

1. What is the right number of customer segments for Liberty?
2. What are their centroids?

CHAPTER 9

Association Rule Mining

Association rule mining is a popular, unsupervised learning technique, used in business to help identify shopping patterns. It is also known as market basket analysis. It helps find interesting relationships (affinities) between variables (items or events). Thus, it can help cross-sell related items and increase the size of a sale.

All data used in this technique is categorical. There is no dependent variable. It uses machine-learning algorithms. The fascinating "relationship between sales of diapers and beers" is how it is often explained in popular literature. This technique accepts as input the raw point-of-sale transaction data. The output produced is the description of the most frequent affinities among items. An example of an association rule would be, "a Customer who bought a laptop computer and virus protection software also bought an extended service plan 70 percent of the time."

Caselet: Netflix—Data Mining in Entertainment

Netflix suggestions and recommendation engines are powered by a suite of algorithms using data about millions of customer ratings about thousands of movies. Most of these algorithms are based on the premise that similar viewing patterns represent similar user tastes. This suite of algorithms, called CineMatch, instructs Netflix's servers to process information from its databases to determine which movies a customer is likely to enjoy. The algorithm takes into account many factors about the films themselves, the customers' ratings, and the combined ratings of all Netflix users. The company estimates that a whopping 75 percent of viewer activity is driven by recommendations. According to Netflix, these predictions were valid around 75 percent of the time and half of Netflix users who rented Cine-Match-recommended movies gave them a five-star rating.

To make matches, a computer

1. *Searches the CineMatch database for people who have rated the same movie—for example, "The Return of the Jedi."*
2. *Determines which of those people have also rated a second movie, such as "The Matrix."*
3. *Calculates the statistical likelihood that people who liked "Return of the Jedi" will also like "The Matrix."*
4. *Continues this process to establish a pattern of correlations between subscribers' ratings of many different films.*

Netflix launched a contest in 2006 to find an algorithm that could beat CineMatch. The contest, called the Netflix Prize, promised $1 million to the first person or team to meet the accuracy goals for recommending movies based on users' personal preferences. Each of these algorithm submissions was required to demonstrate a 10-percent improvement over CineMatch. Three years later, the $1 million prize was awarded to a team of seven people. (source: http://electronics.howstuffworks.com)

Q1. *Are Netflix customers being manipulated into seeing what Netflix wants them to see?*

Q2. *Compare this story with Amazon's personalization engine.*

Business Applications of Association Rules

In business environments a pattern or knowledge can be used for many purposes. In sales and marketing, it is used for cross-marketing and cross-selling, catalog design, e-commerce site design, online advertising optimization, product pricing, and sales/promotion configurations. This analysis can suggest not to put one item on sale at a time, and instead to create a bundle of products promoted as a package to sell other nonselling items.

In retail environments, it can be used for store design. Strongly associated items can be kept close tougher for customer convenience. Or they could be placed far from each other so that the customer has to walk the aisles and by doing so is potentially exposed to other items.

In medicine, this technique can be used for relationships between symptoms and illnesses; diagnosis and patient characteristics/treatments; genes and their functions; and so on.

Representing Association Rules

A generic rule is represented between a set X and Y: $X \Rightarrow Y$ [S%, C%]

X, Y: products and/or services

X: Left-hand-side (LHS or Antecedent)

Y: Right-hand-side (RHS or Consequent)

S: Support: how often **X** and **Y** go together in the total transaction set

C: Confidence: how often **Y** goes together with **X**

Example: {Laptop Computer, Antivirus Software} $\Rightarrow$ {Extended Service Plan} [30%, 70%]

Algorithms for Association Rule

Not all association rules are interesting and useful, only those that are strong rules and also those that occur frequently. In association rule mining, the goal is to find all rules that satisfy the user-specified *minimum support* and *minimum confidence*. The resulting sets of rules are all the same irrespective of the algorithm used, that is, given a transaction data set T, a minimum support and a minimum confidence, the set of association rules existing in T is *uniquely determined*.

Fortunately, there are a large number of algorithms that are available for generating association rules. The most popular algorithms are Apriori, Eclat, and FP-Growth, along with various derivatives and hybrids of the three. All the algorithms help identify the frequent itemsets, which are then converted to association rules.

Apriori Algorithm

This is the most popular algorithm used for association rule mining. The objective is to find subsets that are common to at least a minimum number of the itemsets. A frequent itemset is an itemset whose support is greater than or equal to minimum support threshold. The Apriori property is a downward closure property, which means that any subsets of a frequent itemset are also frequent itemsets. Thus, if (A,B,C,D) is a frequent itemset, then any subset such as (A,B,C) or (B,D) are also frequent itemsets.

This uses a bottom-up approach; and the size of frequent subsets is gradually increased, from one-item subsets to two-item subsets, then three-item subsets, and so on. Groups of candidates at each level are tested against the data for minimum support.

Association Rules Exercise

Here are a dozen sales transactions. There are six products being sold: Milk, Bread, Butter, Eggs, Cookies, and Ketchup. Transaction #1 sold Milk, Eggs, Bread, and Butter. Transaction #2 sold Milk, Butter, Egg, and Ketchup. And so on. The objective is to use this transaction data to find affinities between products, that is, which products sell together often.

The support level will be set at 33 percent; the confidence level will be set at 50 percent. That means that we have decided to consider rules from only those itemsets that occur at least 33 percent of the time in the total set of transactions. Confidence level means that within those itemsets, the rules of the form $X \rightarrow Y$ should be such that there is at least 50 percent chance of Y occurring based on X occurring.

Transactions List				
1	Milk	Egg	Bread	Butter
2	Milk	Butter	Egg	Ketchup
3	Bread	Butter	Ketchup	
4	Milk	Bread	Butter	
5	Bread	Butter	Cookies	
6	Milk	Bread	Butter	Cookies

Transactions List			
7	Milk	Cookies		
8	Milk	Bread	Butter	
9	Bread	Butter	Egg	Cookies
10	Milk	Butter	Bread	
11	Milk	Bread	Butter	
12	Milk	Bread	Cookies	Ketchup

First step is to compute 1-item itemsets, that is, how often any product sells.

1-item Sets	Freq
Milk	9
Bread	10
Butter	10
Egg	3
Ketchup	3
Cookies	5

Thus, Milk sells in 9 out of 12 transactions. Bread sells in 10 out of 12 transactions. And so on.

At every point, there is an opportunity to select itemsets of interest, and thus further analysis. Other itemsets that occur very infrequently may be removed. If itemsets that occur 4 or more times out of 12 are selected, which corresponds to meeting a minimum support level of 33 percent (4 out of 12). Only 4 items make the cut. The frequent items that meet the support level of 33 percent are:

Frequent 1-item Sets	Freq
Milk	9
Bread	10
Butter	10
Cookies	5

The second step is to go for the next level of itemsets using items selected earlier: 2-item itemsets.

2-item Sets	Freq
Milk, Bread	7
Milk, Butter	7
Milk, Cookies	3
Bread, Butter	9
Butter, Cookies	3
Bread, Cookies	4

Thus, (Milk, Bread) sell 7 times out of 12. (Milk, Butter) sell together 7 times, (Bread, Butter) sell together 9 times, and (Bread, Cookies) sell 4 times.

However, only 5 of these transactions meet the minimum support level of 33 percent.

2-item Sets	Freq
Milk, Bread	7
Milk, Butter	7
Bread, Butter	9
Bread, Cookies	4

The next step is to go for the next higher level of itemsets: 3-item itemsets.

3-item Sets	Freq
Milk, Bread, Butter	6
Milk, Bread, Cookies	1
Bread, Butter, Cookies	3

Again, only a subset of them meets the minimum support requirements.

3-item Sets	Freq
Milk, Bread, Butter	6

Thus (Milk, Bread, Butter) sell 6 times out of 12. (Bread, Butter, Cookies) sell 3 times out of 12. There is no room to create a 4-item itemset for this support level.

Creating Association Rules

The most interesting and complex rules at higher size itemsets start top down with the most frequent itemsets of higher size-numbers. Association rules are created that meet the support level (>33 percent) and confidence levels (>50 percent).

The highest level itemset that meets the support requirements is the 3-item itemset. The following itemset has a support level of 50 percent (6 out of 12).

3-item Sets	Freq
Milk, Bread, Butter	6

This itemset could lead to multiple candidate association rules.

Consider the rule: (Bread, Butter) → Milk. Out of total 12 transactions, (Bread, Butter) occurs 9 times; the itemset (Milk, Bread, Butter) occurs 6 times. The rule thus has a support level of 6/12 (or 50 percent) and a confidence level of 6/9 (or 67 percent). The thresholds for the support (>33 percent) and confidence levels (>50 percent) are met. Thus, the first valid association rule from this data is as follows:

1. **(Bread, Butter) → Milk {S = 50%, C = 67%}.**

Consider the rule: (Milk, Bread) → Butter. Out of total 12 transactions, (Milk, Bread) occur 7 times; and (Milk, Bread, Butter) occurs 6 times. The rule has a support level of 6/12 (or 50 percent) and a confidence level of 6/7 (or 84 percent). Thus, the next valid association rule is as follows:

2. **(Milk, Bread) → Butter {S = 50%, C = 84%}.**

Consider the rule: (Milk, Butter) → Bread. Out of total 12 transactions (Milk, Butter) occurs 7 times while (Milk, Bread, Butter) occurs 6 times. The rule has a support level of 7/12 and a confidence level of 6/7 (or 84 percent). Thus, the next valid association rule is as follows:

3. **(Milk, Butter) → Bread {S = 50%, C = 84%}.**

The other high-level itemset that could meet the support requirements is the 3-item itemset

Thus, there are three valid association rules from this data at the 2-itemset values of X, for this support and confidence levels.

If desired, association rules at the 1-item values of X could be specified.

Consider the rule: Milk → Bread. Out of total 12 transactions Milk occurs 9 times while (Milk, Bread) occurs 7 times. The rule has a support level of 7/12 (or 58 percent) and a confidence level of 7/9 (or 77 percent). Thus, the next valid association rule is as follows:

Milk → Bread {S = 58%, C = 77%}.

Many more such rules could be derived if the business requires 1-itemset rules.

The number of association rules depends upon business need. Implementing every rule in business will require some cost and effort, with some potential of gains. The strongest of rules, with the higher support and confidence rates, should be used first, and the others should be progressively implemented later.

Conclusion

Association rules help figure affinities between products in transactions. It helps make cross-selling recommendations much more targeted and effective. Apriori technique is the most popular technique, and it is a machine-learning technique.

Review Exercises

1. What are association rules? How do they help?
2. How many association rules should be used?

Liberty Stores Case Exercise: Step 7

Here is a list of transactions from Liberty's stores. Create association rules for the following data, with 30 percent support level and 60 percent confidence level.

1	A	B	C	E	F	G
2	B	E	F	G		
3	A	C	E	F		
4	B	C	F	G		
5	A	C	E	F	G	
6	C	F	G			
7	A	D	F	G		
8	D	E	F			
9	A	B	D	E		
10	A	B	C	F	G	
11	B	D	E	G		
12	A	C	D	E	F	

SECTION 3

This section covers some additional topics.

Chapter 10 will cover text mining, the art and science of generating insights from text. It is very important in the age of social media.

Chapter 11 will cover web mining, the art and science of generating insights from the World Wide Web, its content and usage. It is very important in the digital age where a lot of advertising and selling is moving to the web.

Chapter 12 will cover Big Data. This is a new moniker created to describe the phenomenon of large amounts of data being generated from many data sources, and which cannot be handled with the traditional data management tools.

Chapter 13 will cover a primer on data modeling. This is useful as a ramp-up to data mining, especially for those who have not had much exposure to traditional data management or may need a refresher.

CHAPTER 10

Text Mining

Text mining is the art and science of discovering knowledge, insights, and patterns from an organized collection of textual databases. Textual mining can help with frequency analysis of important terms and their semantic relationships.

Text is an important part of the growing data in the world. Social media technologies have enabled users to become producers of text and images and other kinds of information. Text mining can be applied to large-scale social media data for gathering preferences and measuring emotional sentiments. It can also be applied to societal, organizational, and individual scales.

Caselet: WhatsApp and Private Security

Do you think that what you post on social media remains private? Think again. A new dashboard shows how much personal information is out there, and how companies are able to construct ways to make use of it for commercial benefits. A dashboard of conversations between two people Jennifer and Nicole over 45 days on whatsapp.

There is a variety of categories that Nicole and Jennifer speak about, such as computers, politics, laundry, and desserts. The polarity of Jennifer's personal thoughts and tone is overwhelmingly positive, and Jennifer responds to Nicole much more than vice versa, identifying Nicole as the influencer in their relationship.

The data visualization reveals the waking hours of Jennifer, showing that she is most active around 8:00 p.m. and heads to bed around midnight. Fifty-three percent of her conversation is about food, and 15 percent about desserts . Maybe she is a strategic person to push restaurant or weight loss ads.

The most intimate detail exposed during this conversation is that Nicole and Jennifer discuss right wing populism, radical parties, and conservative politics. It exemplifies that the amount of private information obtained from your WhatsApp conversations is limitless and potentially dangerous.

WhatsApp is the world's largest messaging service that has over 450 million users. FaceBook recently bought this three-year-old company for a whopping $19 billion. People share a lot of sensitive personal information on WhatsApp that they may not even share with their family members.

(Sources: What Facebook Knows about You from One WhatsApp Conv, by Adi Azaria, on Linked In, April 10, 2014)

> Q1. *What are the business and social implications of this kind of analysis?*
>
> Q2. *Are you worried? Should you be worried?*

Text mining works on texts from practically any kind of sources from any business domains, in any formats, including Word documents, PDF files, XML files, and so on. Here are some representative examples:

1. *In the legal profession:* text sources would include law, court deliberations, court orders, and so on.
2. *In academic research:* it would include texts of interviews, published research articles, and so on.
3. *The world of finance:* will include statutory reports, internal reports, CFO statements, and many more.
4. *In medicine:* it would include medical journals, patient histories, discharge summaries, and so on.
5. *In marketing:* it would include advertisements, customer comments, and so on.
6. *In the world of technology and search:* it would include patent applications, the whole of information on the World Wide Web, and many more.

Text Mining Applications

Text mining is a useful tool in the hands of chief knowledge officers to extract knowledge relevant to an organization. Text mining can be used across industry sectors and application areas, including decision support, sentiment analysis, fraud detection, survey analysis, and many more.

1. *Marketing:* The voice of the customer can be captured in its native and raw format and then analyzed for customer preferences and complaints.

    a. Social personas are a clustering technique to develop customer segments of interest. Consumer input from social media sources, such as reviews, blogs, and tweets, contain numerous leading indicators that can be used toward anticipating and predicting consumer behavior.

    b. A "listening platform" is an application, which in real time, gathers social media, blogs, and other textual feedback, and filters out the chatter to extract true consumer sentiment. The insights can lead to more effective product marketing and better customer service.

    c. The customer call center data can be analyzed for patterns of customer complaints. Decision trees can organize this data to create decision choices that could help with product management activities and to become proactive in avoiding those complaints.

2. *Business operations:*

    a. Social network analysis and text mining can be applied to e-mails, blogs, social media and other data to measure the emotional states and the mood of employee populations. Sentiment analysis can reveal early signs of employee dissatisfaction and this then can be proactively managed.

    b. Studying people as emotional investors and using text analysis of the social Internet to measure mass psychology can help in obtaining superior investment returns.

3. *Legal:* In legal applications, lawyers and paralegals can more easily search case histories and laws for relevant documents in a particular case to improve their chances of winning.

    a. Text mining is also embedded in e-discovery platforms that helps in the process of sharing legally mandated documents.

    b. Case histories, testimonies, and client meeting notes can reveal additional information, such as comorbidities in a health care situation that can help better predict high-cost injuries and prevent costs.

4. *Governance and politics:* Governments can be overturned based on a tweet from a self-immolating fruit-vendor in Tunisia.

   a. Social network analysis and text mining of large-scale social media data can be used for measuring the emotional states and the mood of constituent populations. Microtargeting constituents with specific messages gleaned from social media analysis can be a more efficient use of resources.

   b. In geopolitical security, Internet chatter can be processed for real-time information and to connect the dots on any emerging threats.

   c. In academic, research streams could be meta-analyzed for underlying research trends.

Text Mining Process

Text mining is a semiautomated process. Text data needs to be gathered, structured, and then mined, in a three-step process (Figure 10.1).

1. The text and documents are first gathered into a corpus and organized.
2. The corpus is then analyzed for structure. The result is a matrix mapping important terms to source documents.
3. The structured data is then analyzed for word structures, sequences, and frequency.

Term-document matrix (TDM): This is the heart of the structuring process. Free flowing text can be transformed into numeric data, which can then be mined using regular data mining techniques.

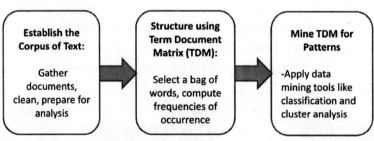

Figure 10.1 Text mining architecture

Table 10.1 Term-document matrix (TDM)

Document/Terms	Term-Document Matrix				
	Investment	Profit	Happy	Success	...
Doc 1	10	4	3	4	
Doc 2	7	2	2		
Doc 3			2	6	
Doc 4	1	5	3		
Doc 5		6		2	
Doc 6	4		2		
...					

1. The technique used for structuring the text is called the bag-of-words technique. This approach measures the frequencies of select important words and/or phrases occurring in each document. This creates a **t × d**, term-by-document matrix (TDM), where t is the number of terms and d is the number of documents.

2. Creating a TDM requires making choices of which terms to include. The terms chosen should reflect the stated purpose of the text mining exercise. The bag of words should be as extensive as needed, but should not include unnecessary stuff that will serve to confuse the analysis or slow the computation (Table 10.1).

Here are some considerations in creating a TDM.

1. A large collection of documents mapped to a large bag of words will likely lead to a very sparse matrix if they have few common words. Reducing dimensionality of data will help improve the speed of analysis and meaningfulness of the results. Synonyms, or terms with similar meaning, should be combined and should be counted together, as a common term. This would help reduce the number of distinct terms of words or "tokens."

2. Data should be cleaned for spelling errors. Common spelling errors should be ignored and the terms should be combined. Uppercase–lowercase terms should also be combined.

3. When many variants of the same term are used, just the stem of the word would be used to reduce the number of terms. For instance, terms

like customer order, ordering, and order data should be combined into a single token word, called "order."

4. On the other side, homonyms (terms with the same spelling but different meanings) should be counted separately. This would enhance the quality of analysis. For example, the term order can mean a customer order, or the ranking of certain choices. These two should be treated separately. "The boss ordered that the customer data analysis be presented in chronological order." This statement shows three different meanings for the word "order." Thus, there will be a need for a manual review of the TDM.

5. Terms with very few occurrences in very few documents should be eliminated from the matrix. This would help increase the density of the matrix and the quality of analysis.

6. The measures in each cell of the matrix could be one of several possibilities. It could be a simple count of the number of occurrences of each term in a document. It could also be the log of that number. It could be the fraction number computed by dividing the frequency count by the total number of words in the document. Or there may be binary values in the matrix to represent whether a term is mentioned or not. The choice of value in the cells will depend upon the purpose of the text analysis.

At the end of this analysis and cleansing, a well-formed, densely populated, rectangular TDM will be ready for analysis. The TDM could be mined using all the available data mining techniques.

Mining the TDM

The TDM can be mined to extract patterns/knowledge. A variety of techniques could be applied to the TDM to extract new knowledge.

Predictors of desirable terms could be discovered through predictive techniques, such as regression analysis. Suppose the word profit is a desirable word in a document. The number of occurrences of the word profit in a document could be regressed against many other terms in the TDM. The relative strengths of the coefficients of various predictor variables would show the relative impact of those terms on creating a profit discussion.

Predicting the chances of a document being liked is another form of analysis. For example, important speeches made by the CEO or the CFO to investors could be evaluated for quality. If the classification of those documents (such as good or poor speeches) was available, then the terms of TDM could be used to predict the speech class. A decision tree could be constructed that makes a simple tree with a few decision points that predicts the success of a speech 80 percent of the time. This tree could be trained with more data to become better over time.

Clustering techniques can help categorize documents by common profile. For example, documents containing the words investment and profit more often could be bundled together. Similarly, documents containing the words, customer orders and marketing, more often could be bundled together. Thus, a few strongly demarcated bundles could capture the essence of the entire TDM. These bundles could thus help with further processing, such as handing over select documents to others for legal discovery.

The association rule analysis could show relationships of coexistence. Thus, one could say that the words, tasty and sweet, occur together often (say 5 percent of the time); and further, when these two words are present, 70 percent of the time, the word happy, is also present in the document.

Comparing Text Mining and Data Mining

Text mining is a form of data mining. There are many common elements between text and data mining. However, there are some key differences. The key difference is that text mining requires conversion of text data into frequency data, before data mining techniques can be applied (Table 10.2).

Text Mining Best Practices

Many of the same best practices that apply to the use of data mining techniques will also apply to text mining.

1. The first and most important practice is to ask the right question. A good question is one which gives an answer and would lead to

Table 10.2 Comparing text and data mining

Dimension	Text Mining	Data Mining
Nature of data	Unstructured data: words, phrases, sentences	Numbers; alphabetical and logical values
Language used	Many languages and dialects used in the world; many languages are extinct, new documents are discovered	Similar numerical systems across the world
Clarity and precision	Sentences can be ambiguous; sentiment may contradict the words	Numbers are precise
Consistency	Different parts of the text can contradict each other	Different parts of data can be inconsistent, thus, requiring statistical significance analysis
Sentiment	Text may present a clear and consistent or mixed sentiment, across a continuum. Spoken words adds further sentiment	N/A
Quality	Spelling errors. Differing values of proper nouns, such as names. Varying quality of language translation	Issues with missing values, outliers, and so on
Nature of analysis	Keyword-based search; coexistence of themes; sentiment mining	A full wide range of statistical and machine-learning analysis for relationships and differences

large payoffs for the organization. The purpose and the key question will define how and at what levels of granularity the TDM would be made. For example, TDM defined for simpler searches would be different from those used for complex semantic analysis or network analysis.

2. A second important practice is to be creative and open in proposing imaginative hypotheses for the solution. Thinking outside the box is important, both in the quality of the proposed solution as well as in finding the high-quality data sets required to test the hypothesized solution. For example, a TDM of consumer sentiment data should be combined with customer order data in order to develop

a comprehensive view of customer behavior. It is important to assemble a team that has a healthy mix of technical and business skills.

3. Another important element is to go after the problem iteratively. Too
   much data can overwhelm the infrastructure and also befuddle the
   mind. It is better to divide and conquer the problem with a simpler
   TDM, with fewer terms and fewer documents and data sources. Expand as needed, in an iterative sequence of steps. In the future, add
   new terms to help improve predictive accuracy.

4. A variety of data mining tools should be used to test the relationships
   in the TDM. Different decision tree algorithms could be run along-
   side cluster analysis and other techniques. Triangulating the findings
   with multiple techniques, and many what-if scenarios, helps build
   confidence in the solution. Test the solution in many ways before
   committing to it.

Conclusion

Text mining is diving into the unstructured text to discover valuable in-
sights about the business. The text is gathered and then structured into a
TDM based on the frequency of a bag of words in a corpus of documents.
The TDM can then be mined for useful, novel patterns, and insights.
While the technique is important, the business objective should be well
understood and should always be kept in mind.

Review Questions

1. Why is text mining useful in the age of social media?
2. What kinds of problems can be addressed using text mining?
3. What kinds of sentiments can be found in the text?

Liberty Stores Case Exercise: Step 8

Here are a few comments from customer service calls received by Liberty.

1. *I loved the design of the shirt. The size fitted me very well. However, the fabric seemed flimsy. I am calling to see if you can replace the shirt with a different one. Or please refund my money.*
2. *I was running late from work, and I stopped by to pick up some groceries. I did not like the way the manager closed the store while I was still shopping.*
3. *I stopped by to pick up flowers. The checkout line was very long. The manager was polite but did not open new cashiers. I got late for my appointment.*

4. *The manager promised that the product will be there, but when I went there the product was not there. The visit was a waste. The manager should have compensated me for my trouble.*
5. *When there was a problem with my catering order, the store manager promptly contacted me and quickly got the kinks out to send me replacement food immediately. They are very courteous.*

Create a TDM with not more than six key terms. [Hint: Treat each comment as a document.]

CHAPTER 11

Web Mining

Web mining is the art and science of discovering patterns and insights from the World Wide Web so as to improve it. The World Wide Web is at the heart of the digital revolution. More data is posted on the Web every day than was there on the whole Web just 20 years ago. Billions of users are using it every day for a variety of purposes. The Web is used for e-commerce, business communication, and many other applications. Web mining analyzes data from the Web and helps find insights that could optimize the web content and improve the user experience. Data for web mining is collected via web crawlers, web logs, and other means.

Here are some characteristics of optimized websites:

1. *Appearance:* Aesthetic design; well-formatted content, easy to scan and navigate; and good color contrasts.
2. *Content:* Well-planned information architecture with useful content; fresh content; search-engine optimized; and links to other good sites.
3. *Functionality:* Accessible to all authorized users; fast loading times; usable forms; and mobile enabled.

This type of content and its structure are of interest to ensure that the Web is easy to use. The analysis of web usage provides feedback on the web content and also the consumer's browsing habits. This data can be of immense use for commercial advertising, and even for social engineering.

The Web could be analyzed for its structure as well as content. The usage pattern of web pages could also be analyzed. Depending upon objectives, web mining can be divided into three different types: web usage mining, web content mining, and web structure mining (Figure 11.1).

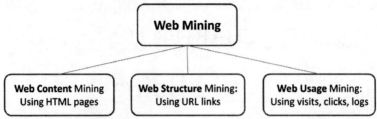

Figure 11.1 Web mining structure

Web Content Mining

A website is designed in the form of pages with a distinct URL (universal resource locator). A large website may contain thousands of pages. Those pages and their content are managed using content management systems. Every page can have text, graphics, audio, video, forms, applications, and more kinds of content, including user-generated content. The websites make a record of all requests received for its page/URLs. The log of these requests could be analyzed to gauge the popularity of those pages. The textual and application content could be analyzed for its usage by visits to the website. The pages on a website themselves could be analyzed for quality of content. The unwanted pages could be transformed with different content and style, or they may be deleted altogether. Similarly, more resources could be assigned to keep the more popular pages more fresh and inviting.

Web Structure Mining

The Web works through a system of hyperlinks using the hypertext protocol (http). Any page can create a link to any other page. The intertwined or self-referral nature of the Web lends itself to some unique analytical algorithms. The structure of web pages could also be analyzed to examine the structure of hyperlinks among pages. There are two basic strategic models for successful websites: hubs and authorities.

1. *Hubs:* The pages with a large number of interesting links would serve as a hub, or a gathering point, where people access a variety of information. Media sites like Yahoo.com or government sites would serve

that purpose. There are focused hubs like Traveladvisor.com and many websites which could aspire to become hubs for new emerging areas.

2. *Authorities:* Ultimately, people would gravitate toward pages that provide the most complete and authoritative information on a particular subject, including user reviews. These websites would have the most number of inbound links. Thus, Mayoclinic.com would serve as an authoritative page for expert medical opinion.

Web Usage Mining

As a user clicks anywhere on a web page or application, the action is recorded by many entities in many locations. The browser at the client machine will record the click, and the web server providing the content would also log onto the pages-served activity. The entities between the client and the server, such as the router, proxy server, or ad server, too, would record that click.

The goal of web usage is to extract useful information from data generated through web page visits and transactions. The activity data comes from data stored in server access logs, referrer logs, agent logs, and client-side cookies. The user characteristics and usage profiles are also gathered directly, or indirectly, through syndicated data. Further, metadata, such as page attributes, content attributes, and usage data, are also gathered.

The web content could be analyzed at multiple levels.

1. The server side analysis would show the relative popularity of the web pages accessed. Those websites could be hubs and authorities.
2. The client-side analysis could focus on the usage pattern or the actual content consumed and created by users.
   a. Usage pattern could be analyzed using "clickstream" analysis, that is, analyzing web activity for patterns of sequence of clicks, and the location and duration of visits on websites. Clickstream analysis is useful for web activity analysis, software testing, market research, and analyzing employee productivity.
   b. Textual information accessed on the pages retrieved by users could be analyzed using text mining techniques. The text would be gathered and structured using the bag-of-words technique to build a

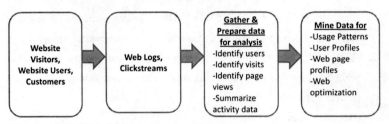

Figure 11.2 Web usage mining architecture

term-document matrix. This matrix could then be mined using cluster analysis and association rules for patterns, such as popular topics, user segmentation, and sentiment analysis (Figure 11.2).

It can help predict user behavior based on previously learned rules and users' profiles, and can help determine lifetime value of clients. It can also help design cross-marketing strategies across products, by observing association rules among the pages on the website. Web usage can help evaluate promotional campaigns and see if the users were attracted to the website and used the pages relevant to the campaign.

Web usage could be used to present dynamic information to users based on their interests and profiles. This includes targeted online ads and coupons at user groups based on user access patterns.

Web Mining Algorithms

Hyperlink-Induced Topic Search (HITS) is a link analysis algorithm that rates web pages as being hubs or authorities. Many other HITS-based algorithms have also been published. The most famous and powerful of these algorithms is the PageRank algorithm. Invented by Google co-founder Larry Page, this algorithm is used by Google to organize the results of its search function. This algorithm helps determine the relative importance of any particular web page by counting the number and quality of links to a page. The websites with more number of links, and/or more links from higher-quality websites, will be ranked higher. It works similar to determining the status of a person in a society of people. Those with relations to more people and/or relations to people of higher status will be accorded a higher status.

PageRank is the algorithm that helps determine the order of pages listed upon a Google Search query. The original algorithm has been updated in many ways and the latest algorithm is kept a secret so that other websites cannot take advantage of the algorithm and manipulate their website according to it. However, there are many standard elements that remain unchanged. These elements lead to the principles for a good website. This process is also called search-engine optimization (SEO).

Conclusion

The Web has growing resources, with more content every day and more users visiting it for many purposes. A good website should be useful, easy to use, and flexible for evolution. From the insights gleaned using web mining, websites should be constantly optimized.

Web usage mining can help discover what content users really like and censure, and help prioritize that for improvement. Web structure can help improve traffic to those sites, by building authority for the sites.

Review Questions

1. What are the three types of web mining?
2. What is clickstream analysis?
3. What are the two major ways that a website can become popular?
4. What are the privacy issues in web mining?
5. A user spends 60 minutes on the web, visiting 10 web pages in all. Given the clickstream data, what kind of an analysis would you do?

CHAPTER 12

Big Data

Big data is an umbrella term for a collection of data sets so large and complex that it becomes difficult to process them using traditional data management tools. There has been increasing democratization of the process of content creation and sharing over the Internet, using social media applications. The combination of cloud-based storage, social media applications, and mobile access devices is helping crystallize the big data phenomenon. The leading management consulting firm, McKinsey & Co. created a flutter when it published a report in 2011 showing the impact of such big data on organizations. They reported that there will be millions of new jobs in the next decade, related to the use of big data in many industries.

Big data can be used to discover new insights from a 360-degree view of a situation that can allow for a complete new perspective on situations, new models of reality, and potentially new types of solutions. It can help spot business trends and opportunities. For example, Google is able to predict the spread of a disease by tracking the use of search terms related to the symptoms of the disease over the globe in real time. Big data can help determine the quality of research, prevent diseases, link legal citations, combat crime, and determine real-time roadway traffic conditions. Big data is enabling evidence-based medicine and many other innovations.

Data has become the new natural resource. Organizations have a choice in how to engage with this exponentially growing volume, variety, and velocity of data. They can choose to be buried under the avalanche, or they can choose to use it for competitive advantage. Challenges in big data include the entire range of operations from capture, curation, storage, search, sharing, analysis, and visualization. Big data is more valuable when analyzed as a whole. More and more information is derivable from analysis of a single large set of related data, as compared to separate smaller sets. However, special tools and skills are needed to manage such extremely large data sets.

Caselet: Personalized Promotions at Sears

A couple of years ago, Sears Holdings came to the conclusion that it needed to generate greater value from the huge amounts of customer, product, and promotion data it collected from its many brands. Sears required about eight weeks to generate personalized promotions, at which point many of them were no longer optimal for the company. It took so long mainly because the data required for these large-scale analyses were both voluminous and highly fragmented—housed in many databases and "data warehouses" maintained by the various brands. Sears turned to the technologies and practices of big data. As one of its first steps, it set up a Hadoop cluster, using a group of inexpensive commodity servers.

Sears started using the Hadoop cluster to store incoming data from all its brands and from existing data warehouses. It then conducted analyses on the cluster directly, avoiding the time-consuming complexities of pulling data from various sources and combining them so that they can be analyzed. Sears's Hadoop cluster stores and processes several petabytes of data at a fraction of the cost of a comparable standard data warehouse. The time needed to generate a comprehensive set of promotions dropped from eight weeks to one. And these promotions are of higher quality, because they are more timely, more granular, and more personalized. (Source: McAfee and Brynjolfsson HBS Oct 2012)

Q1. *What are other ways in which Sears can benefit from big data?*

Q2. *What are the challenges in making use of big data?*

Defining Big Data

In 2000, there were 800,000 petabytes of data in the world. It is expected to grow to 35 zettabytes by the year 2020. About half a million books worth of data is being created daily on social media alone.

Big data is big, fast, unstructured, and of many types. There are several unique features:

1. *Variety:* There are many types of data, including structured and unstructured data. Structured data consists of numeric and text fields. Unstructured data includes images, video, audio, and many other types. There are also many sources of data. The traditional sources of structured data include data from ERPs systems and other operational systems. Sources for unstructured data include social media, Web, RFID, machine data, and others. Unstructured data comes in a variety of sizes, resolutions, and are subject to different kinds of analysis. For example, video files can be tagged with labels, and they can be played, but video data is typically not computed, which is the same with audio data. Graphic data can be analyzed for network distances. Facebook texts and tweets can be analyzed for sentiments, but cannot be directly compared.

2. *Velocity:* The Internet greatly increases the speed of movement of data, from e-mails to social media to video files, data can move quickly. Cloud computing makes sharing instantaneous, and easily accessible from anywhere. Social media applications enable people to share their data with each other instantly. Mobile access to these applications also speeds up the generation and access to data (Figure 12.1).

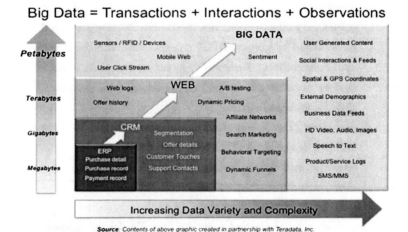

Figure 12.1 Sources of big data

(Source: Hortonworks.com)

3. *Volume:* Websites have become great repositories for all kinds of data. User clickstreams are recorded and stored for future use. Social media applications such as Facebook, Twitter, Pinterest, and other applications have enabled users to become prosumers of data (producers and consumers). There is an increase in the number of data shares, and also the size of each data elements. High-definition videos can increase the total shared data. There are autonomous data streams of video, audio, text, data, and so on coming from social media sites, websites, RFID applications, and so on.

4. *Sources of data:* There are several sources of data, including some new ones. Data from outside the organization may be incomplete and of an indifferent quality.

   a. People: All activities on the Web and social media are considered stores and are accessible. E-mail was the first major source of new data. Google searches, Facebook posts, Tweets, Youtube videos, other social media, and blogs enable people to generate data for one another.

   b. Organizations: Business organizations and government are major generators of data. ERP systems, e-commerce systems, user-generated content, web-access logs, and many other sources of data generate valuable data for organizations.

   c. Machines: The Internet of things is evolving. Many machines are connected to the network and autonomously generate data that is not touched by human. RFID tags and telematics are two major applications that generate enormous amounts of data. Connected devices, such as phones and refrigerators, generate data about their location and status.

   d. Metadata: There is enormous data about data itself. Web crawlers and web-bots scan the Web to capture new web pages, their html structure, and their metadata. This data is used by many applications, including web search engines.

The data also includes varied quality of data. Data from within the organization is likely to be of a higher quality. Publicly available data would include some trustworthy data, along with data that is less so.

Big Data Landscape

Big data can be understood at many levels. At the highest level are business applications to suit particular industries or to suit business intelligence for executives. A unique concept of "data as a service" is also possible for particular industries. At the next level, there are infrastructure elements for broad cross-industry applications, such as analytics and structured databases. This also includes offering this infrastructure as a service with some operational management services built in. At the core, it is about technologies and standards to store and manipulate the large fast streams of data.

Business Implications of Big Data

Big data is disrupting every industry. Any industry that produces information-based products is most likely to be disrupted. Thus, the newspaper industry has taken a hit from digital distribution, as well as from published-on-web-only blogs. Entertainment has also been impacted by digital distribution and piracy, as well as by user-generated-and-uploaded content on the Internet. The education industry is being disrupted by massively online open courses (MOOCs) and user-uploaded content. Health care delivery is impacted by electronic health records and digital medicine. The retail industry has been massively disrupted by e-commerce companies. Fashion companies are impacted by quick feedback on social media. The banking industry has been impacted by the cost-effective online banking system, and this will impact employment levels in the industry.

There is rapid change in business models enabled by big data technologies. Steve Jobs, the ex-CEO of Apple, conceded that his company's products would be disrupted. He preferred them to be cannibalized by his own products rather than by those of the competition.

Every business too will be disrupted. The key business issue for business is how to harness big data for business to generate growth opportunities and to leapfrog competition. Organizations need to figure out how to use generated data as a strategic asset in real time, to identify opportunities, thwart threats, and achieve operational efficiencies. Organizations need to learn how to organize their businesses so that they do not get buried in high volume, velocity, and the variety of data, but instead use it smartly and proactively to obtain a quick "2-second advantage" over their competition to get to the opportunity first. Organizations can now effectively fuse strategy and digital business, and then strive to design innovative "digital business strategy" around digital assets and capabilities.

Technology Implications of Big Data

Organizations are now compelled to address the variety of information assets they have access to, and how they process and make use of them. At the same time, the demands for information are constantly changing as the business models continue to evolve.

The growth of data is made possible in part by the advancement of storage technology. The attached graph shows the growth of disk-drive average capacities. The cost of storage is falling, the size of storage is getting smaller, and the speed of access is going up. Flash drives are become cheaper. Random access memory storage used to be expensive, but now is so inexpensive that entire databases can be loaded and processed quickly, instead of swapping data in and out of memory.

New data management and processing technologies have emerged. IT professionals integrate "big data" structured assets with content and must increase their business requirement identification skills. Big data is going democratic. Business functions will be protective of their data and will begin initiatives around exploiting it. IT support teams need to find ways to support end-user-deployed big data solutions. Enterprise data warehouses will need to include big data in some form. The IT platform needs to be strengthened to help provide the enablement of a "digital business strategy" around digital assets and capabilities.

Big Data Technologies

New tools and techniques have arisen in the last 10 to 20 years to handle this large and still growing data. There are technologies for storing and accessing this data.

1. *Nonrelational data structures:* Big data is stored using nontraditional data structures. Large nonrelational databases like Hadoop have

emerged as a leading data management platform for big data. In Hadoop's Distributed File System (HDFS), data is stored as "key and data-value" combinations. Google BigFile is another prominent technology. NoSQL is emerging as a language to manage nonrelational databases. The open-sourced stack of programing languages (such as Pig and Hive) and other tools help make Hadoop a powerful and popular tool.

2. *Massively parallel computing:* Given the size of data, it is useful to divide and conquer the problem quickly using multiple processors simultaneously. Parallel processing allows for the data to be processed by multiple machines so that results can be achieved sooner. MapReduce algorithm, originally generated at Google for doing searches faster, has emerged as a popular parallel processing mechanism. The original problem is divided into smaller problems, which are then mapped to multiple processors that can operate in parallel. The outputs of these processors are passed to an output processor that reduces the output to a single stream, which is then sent to the end user. Here is an example of a MapReduce algorithm (Figure 12.2).

3. Unstructured Information Management Architecture (UIMA). This is the "secret sauce" behind IBM' Watson's system that reads massive amounts of data, and organizes for just-in-time processing. Watson beat the Jeopardy (quiz program) champion in 2011 and is now used for many business applications, like diagnosis, in health care situations. Natural language processing is another capability that helps extend the power of big data technologies.

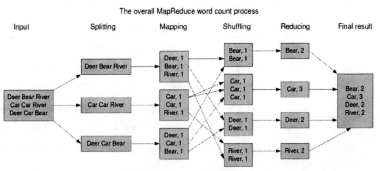

Figure 12.2 A MapReduce parallel processing algorithm example (source: www.cs.uml.edu)

Management of Big Data

Many organizations have started initiatives around the use of big data. However, most organizations do not necessarily have a grip on it. Here are some emerging insights into making better use of big data.

1. Across all industries, the business case for big data is strongly focused on addressing customer-centric objectives. The first focus on deploying big data initiatives is to protect and enhance customer relationships and customer experience.

2. A scalable and extensible information management foundation is a prerequisite for big data advancement. Big data builds upon resilient, secure, efficient, flexible, and real-time information processing environment.

3. Organizations are beginning their pilots and implementations by using existing and newly accessible internal sources of data. It is better to begin with data under one's control and where one has a superior understanding of the data.

4. Advanced analytical capabilities are required, yet lacking, for organizations to get the most value from big data. There is a growing awareness of building or hiring those skills and capabilities.

5. The faster you analyze the data, the more its predictive value. The value of data depreciates with time. If the data is not processed in five minutes, then an immediate advantage is lost.

6. Maintain one copy of your data, not multiple. This would help avoid confusion and increase efficiency.

7. Use more diverse data, not just more data. This would provide a broader perspective into reality and better quality insights.

8. Data has value beyond what you initially anticipate. Do not throw away data if no immediate use can be seen for it. Data can add perspective to other data in a multiplicative manner.

9. Plan for exponential growth. Data is expected to continue to grow at exponential rates. Storage costs continue to fall, data generation continues to grow, and data-based applications continue to grow in capability and functionality.

10. Solve a real pain-point. Big data should be deployed for specific business objectives in order to avoid being overwhelmed by the sheer size of it all.

11. Put humans and data together to get the most insight. Combining data-based analysis with human intuition and perspectives is better than going just one way.

12. Big data is transforming business, just like IT did. Big data is a new phase representing a digital world. Business and society are not immune to its strong impacts.

Conclusion

Big data is a new natural force and natural resource. The exponentially growing volume, variety, and velocity of data are constantly disrupting businesses across all industries, at multiple levels from product to business models. Organizations need to begin initiatives around big data; acquire skills, tools, and technologies; and show the vision to disrupt their industry and come out ahead.

Review Questions

1. What are the three Vs of big data?
2. How does big data impact the business models?
3. What is Hadoop?
4. How does MapReduce algorithm work?
5. What are the key issues in managing big data?

CHAPTER 13

Data Modeling Primer

Data needs to be efficiently structured and stored so that it includes all the information needed for decision making, without duplication and loss of integrity. Here are top 10 qualities of good data.

Data should be:

1. *Accurate:* Data should retain consistent values across data stores, users and applications. This is the most important aspect of data. Any use of inaccurate or corrupted data to do any analysis is known as the garbage-in-garbage-out (GIGO) condition.
2. *Persistent:* Data should be available for all times, now and later. It should thus be nonvolatile, stored and managed for later access.
3. *Available:* Data should be made available to authorized users, when, where, and how they want to access it, within policy constraints.
4. *Accessible:* Not only should data be available to user, it should also be easy to use. Thus, data should be made available in desired formats, with easy tools. MS Excel is a popular medium to access numeric data, and then transfer to other formats.
5. *Comprehensive:* Data should be gathered from all relevant sources to provide a complete and holistic view of the situation. New dimensions should be added to data as and when they become available.
6. *Analyzable:* Data should be available for analysis, for historical and predictive purposes. Thus, data should be organized such that it can be used by analytical tools, such as OLAP, data cube, or data mining.
7. *Flexible:* Data is growing in variety of types. Thus, data stores should be able to store a variety of data types: small/large, text/video, and so on
8. *Scalable:* Data is growing in volume. Data storage should be organized to meet emergent demands.

9. *Secure:* Data should be doubly and triply backed up, and protected against loss and damage. There is no bigger IT nightmare than corrupted data. Inconsistent data has to be manually sorted out which leads to loss of face, loss of business, downtime, and sometimes the business never recovers.

10. *Cost-effective:* The cost of collecting data and storing it is coming down rapidly. However, still the total cost of gathering, organizing, and storing a type of data should be proportional to the estimated value from its use.

Evolution of Data Management Systems

Data management has evolved from manual filing systems to the most advanced online systems capable of handling millions of data processing and access requests each second.

The first data management systems were called file systems. These mimicked paper files and folders. Everything was stored chronologically. Access to this data was sequential.

The next step in data modeling was to find ways to access any random record quickly. Thus, hierarchical database systems appeared. They were able to connect all items for an order, given an order number.

The next step was to traverse the linkages both ways, from top of the hierarchy to the bottom, and from the bottom to the top. Given an item sold, one should be able to find its order number, and list all the other items sold in that order. Thus, there were networks of links established in the data to track those relationships.

The major leap came when the relationship between data elements itself became the center of attention. The relationship between data values was the key element of storage. Relationships were established through matching values of common attributes, rather than by location of the record in a file. This led to data modeling using relational algebra. Relations could be joined and subtracted, with set operations like union and intersection. Searching the data became an easier task by declaring the values of a variable of interest.

The relational model was enhanced to include variables with noncomparable values like binary objects (such as pictures), which had to be processed differently. Thus emerged the idea of encapsulating the procedures along with the data elements they worked on. The data and its methods were encapsulated into an "object." Those objects could be further specialized. For example, a vehicle was an object with certain attributes. A car and a truck were more specialized versions of a vehicle. They inherited the data structure of the vehicle, but had their own additional attributes. Similarly, the specialized object inherited all the procedures and programs associated with the more general entity. This became the object-oriented model.

Relational Data Model

The first mathematical-theory-driven model for data management was designed by Ed Codd in 1970.

1. A relational database is composed of a set of relations (data tables), which can be joined using shared attributes. A "data table" is a collection of instances (or records), with a key attribute to uniquely identify each instance.
2. Data tables can be JOINed using the shared "key" attributes to create larger temporary tables, which can be queried to fetch information across tables. Joins can be simple as between two tables. Joins can also be complex with AND, OR, UNION or INTERSECTION, and more of many joins.
3. High-level commands in Structured Query Language (SQL) can be used to perform joins, selection, and organizing of records.

Relational data models flow from conceptual models, to logical models to physical implementations.

Data can be conceived of as being about entities, and relationships among entities. A relationship between entities may be hierarchy between entities, or transactions involving multiple entities. These can be graphically represented as an entity–relationship diagram (ERD).

1. An **entity** is any object or event about which someone chooses to collect data, which may be a person, place, or thing (e.g., sales person, city, product, vehicle, employee).

2. Entities have **attributes**. Attributes are data items that have something in common with the entity. For example, student id, student name, and student address represent details for a student entity. Attributes can be single-valued (e.g., student name) or multi-valued (list of past addresses for the student). Attribute can be simple (e.g., student name) or composite (e.g., student address, composed of street, city, and state).

3. **Relationships** have many characteristics: degree, cardinality, and participation.

4. **Degree of relationship** depends upon the number of entities participating in a relationship. Relationships can be unary (e.g., employee and manager-as-employee), binary (e.g., student and course), and ternary (e.g., vendor, part, warehouse)

5. **Cardinality** represents the extent of participation of each entity in a relationship.

   a. One-to-one (e.g., employee and parking space)

   b. One-to-many (e.g., customer and orders)

   c. Many-to-many (e.g., student and course)

6. **Participation** indicates the optional or mandatory nature of relationship.

   a. Customer and order (mandatory)

   b. Employee and course (optional)

7. There are also **weak entities** that are dependent on another entity for its existence (e.g., employees and dependents). If an employee data is removed, then the dependent data must also be removed.

8. There are **associative entities** used to represent M–N relationships (e.g., student-course registration).

9. There are also **super sub type entities**. These help represent additional attributes, on a subset of the records. For example, vehicle is a supertype and passenger car is its subtype.

In Figure 13.1, the rectangle reflects the entities students and courses. The relationship is enrolment.

Every entity must have a key attribute(s) that can be used to identify an instance. For example, student ID can identify a student. A primary key is a unique attribute value for the instance (e.g., student ID). Any attribute that can serve as a primary key (e.g., student address) is a

Figure 13.1 Sample relationship between two entities

candidate key. A secondary key—a key which may not be unique—may be used to select a group of records (student city).

Some entities will have a composite key—a combination of two or more attributes that together uniquely represent the key (e.g., flight number and flight date).

A foreign key is useful in representing a one-to-many relationship. The primary key of the file at the one end of the relationship should be contained as a foreign key on the file at the many end of the relationship.

A many-to-many relationship creates the need for an associative entity. There are two ways to implement it. It could be converted into two one-to-many relationships with an associative entity in the middle. Alternatively, the combination of primary keys of the entities participating in the relationship will form the primary key for the associative entity.

Implementing the Relational Data Model

Once the logical data model has been created, it is easy to implement it using a DBMS.

Every entity should be implemented by creating a database table. Every table will be a specific data field (key) that would uniquely identify each relation (or row) in that table. Each master table or database relation should have programs to create, read, update, and delete the records.

The databases should follow three integrity constraints.

1. **Entity integrity** ensures that the entity or a table is healthy. The primary key cannot have a null value. Every row must have a unique value, or else that row should be deleted. As a corollary, if the primary key is a composite key, none of the fields participating in the key can contain a null value. Every key must be unique.
2. **Domain integrity** is enforced by using rules to validate the data as being of the appropriate range and type.

3. **Referential integrity** governs the nature of records in a one-to-many relationship. This ensures that the value of a foreign key should have a matching value in primary keys of the table referred to by the foreign key.

Database Management Systems

These are many software packages that manage the background activities related to storing the relations, the data itself, and doing the operations on the relations. The data in the DBMS grows, and it serves many users of the data concurrently. The DBMS typically runs on a machine called a database server—in an n-tier web-application architecture. Thus in an airline reservation system, millions of transactions might simultaneously try to access the same set of data. The database is constantly managed to provide data access to all authorized users, securely and speedily, while keeping the database consistent and useful. Content management systems help people manage their own data that goes out on a website. There are object-oriented and other more complex ways of managing data, some of which were covered in Chapter 12.

Conclusion

Data should be modeled to achieve the business objectives. Good data should be accurate and accessible so that it can be used for business operations. Relational data model is the two most popular way of managing data today.

Review Questions

1. Who invented relational model and when?
2. How does relational model mark a clear break from previous database models?
3. What is an entity–relationship diagram?
4. What kinds of attributes can an entity have?
5. What are the different kinds of relationships?

Additional Resources

Join Teradata University Network to access tools and materials for Business Intelligence. It is completely free for students.

Here are some other books and papers for a deeper dive into the topics covered in this book.

Andrew D. Martin et al. "Competing Approaches to Predicting Supreme Court Decision making." *Perspective in Politics* (2004).

Ayres, Ian. *Super Crunchers: Why Thinking-by-Numbers Is the New Way to Be Smart.* Random House Publishing, 2007.

Davenport, Thomas H., and Jeanne G. Harris. *Competing on Analytics: The New Science of Winning.* HBS Press, 2007.

Gordon, Linoff S., and Michael Berry *Data Mining Techniques.* 3rd ed. Wiley, 2011.

Groebner, David F., Patrick W. Shannon, and Philip C. Fry. *Business Statistics.* 9th ed. Pearson, 2013.

Jain, Anil K. "Data Clustering: 50 Years Beyond K-Means." In *19th International Conference on Pattern Recognition.* 2008.

Lewis, Michael. *Moneyball: The Art of Winning an Unfair Game.* Norton & Co, 2004.

Mayer-Schonberger, Viktor, and Kenneth Cukier. *Big Data: A Revolution That Will Transform How We Live, Work, and Think.* Houghton Mifflin Harcourt, 2013.

McKinsey Global Institute Report. "Big data: The next frontier for innovation, competition, and productivity." http://www.Mckinsey.com. 2011.

Sathi, Arvind. *Customer Experience Analytics: The Key to Real-Time, Adaptive Customer Relationships.* Independent Publishers Group, 2011.

Sharda, Ramesh, Dursun Delen, and Turban Efraim. *Business Intelligence and Data Analytics.* 10th ed. Pearson, 2014.

Shmueli, Galit, Nitin Patel, and Peter Bruce. *Data Mining for Business Intelligence.* Wiley, 2010.

Siegel, Eric. *Predictive Analytics.* Wiley, 2013.

Silver, Nate. *The Signal and the Noise: Why So Many Predictions Fail but Some Don't.* Penguin Press, 2012.

Statsoft. http://www.statsoft/textbook.

Taylor, James. *Decision Management Systems: A Practical Guide to Using Business Rules and Predictive Analytics*. Pearson Education (IBM Press), 2011.

Weka system. http://www.cs.waikato.ac.nz/ml/weka/downloading.html.

Witten, Ian, Eibe Frank, and Mark Hall. *Data Mining*. 3rd ed. Morgan Kauffman, 2009.

Index

FORTHCOMING TITLES IN OUR BIG DATA AND BUSINESS ANALYTICS COLLECTION

Mark Ferguson, University of South Carolina, Editor

- *An Introduction to Big Data, Data Mining, and Text Mining* by Barry Keating
- *Business Location Analytics: The Research and Marketing Strategic Advantage* by David Z. Beitz

Announcing the Business Expert Press Digital Library

Concise e-books business students need for classroom and research

This book can also be purchased in an e-book collection by your library as

- a one-time purchase,
- that is owned forever,
- allows for simultaneous readers,
- has no restrictions on printing, and
- can be downloaded as PDFs from within the library community.

Our digital library collections are a great solution to beat the rising cost of textbooks. e-books can be loaded into their course management systems or onto student's e-book readers.
The **Business Expert Press** digital libraries are very affordable, with no obligation to buy in future years. For more information, please visit **www.businessexpertpress.com/librarians.** To set up a trial in the United States, please contact **Adam Chesler** at adam.chesler@businessexpertpress.com. For all other regions, contact **Nicole Lee** at nicole.lee@igroupnet.com.